The One Person Business

EVERYTHING YOU NEED TO KNOW FROM STARTUP TO SUCCESS

By Lee Simon

© Lee Simon 2013
All rights reserved.

ISBN: 1494231409
ISBN 13: 9781494231408

Library of Congress Control Number: 2013922440
CreateSpace Independent Publishing Platform
North Charleston, South Carolina

Table of Contents

Introduction vii

Making Your Decision. 1
Is it right for you? 12 Ways to see if it is - Start One-Buy One - Buy a Franchise - Is your idea viable?

Steps to Success . . . .
7 steps to success - 10 most common mistakes - 16 more mistakes to avoid - 4 risk factors to consider - Dealing with your fears - 7 Keys to small business success - 11 negotiating tips

Getting It Started . . . .
Locating your business - How to legitimize it - Setting your business goals - To-Do list for startups - The money to start it - Projections and tracking the money

Marketing. 27
General marketing factors - Demographics of prospective buyers - 14 marketing temptations to avoid - Your marketing strategy - Your marketing

plan - Getting customers - What do you really sell? Positioning in your marketplace - Reaching your target market - 74 tips on website and social media marketing - Creating your brand - Your image in the marketplace - Writing a great headline - Competitive advantage (CA) - Words to use/not use in marketing - Graphic design factors - Your logo - Naming your business - Your slogan (tag) - Pricing your product/service

Sales 59

Sales Strategies - Your sales plan - Your sales process - 6 sales maxims - 28 street-smart sales tips - 14 sales No-No's - Body Language In Closing the Sale - Closing the sale - 31 reasons why there was no sale - Handling Objections - Asking Questions - Listening tips - Rating your customers - Assessing your sales results

Operations 91

Systematizing your small business - What to systematize - Work flow - Guides to systemization

Administration 95

Support for the other components - outsourcing tasks

Finance 97

3 Projections to make - Budget projections - Sales projections - Cash flow projections - Calculating breakeven - Financial analysis - Money advice - Collecting money customers owe you - Guide to borrowing money

Conclusion 115

Appendices

A. All About Buying an Existing Business 117
B. All About Buying a Franchise 127
C. 10 Myths About Owning a One Person Business 143
D. 11 Reasons Why Small Businesses Fail 145
E. 8 Website Mistakes to Avoid 147
F. 10 Traps to Avoid 149
G. 36 Ways to Check out Your Idea 153
H. Locating Your Business 163
I. Startup Costs 169
J. Direct Mail Marketing 171
K. Marketing Plan 173
L. 51 Tips for Retail 177
M. Types of Customers 183
N. Tracking Your Results 185
O. Profit Margins Explained 191
P. Business Plan 193
Q. Selling Online 199
R. Handling Buyer Objections 201
S. Service Business Tips 205
T. Home-based Business 207
U. Tax-Deductible Expenses 209

Introduction

A one-person business is just that, only one owner, one manager, and one worker, in all three roles. It can be a sole proprietorship, an LLC, or a home-based business. You may sell a product or a service. If it's a service business, your service is your product (See Appendix S for tips for service businesses).

For the first year or so most one person businesses stay one person, then if they are making enough money, the first employee is hired, but it may stay a one person business forever, and that's perfectly fine.

If I had only this book (and enough money) I could start and run a successful one-person business. So will you.

There are lots of advantages to being a one-person business. And, if you do become a one+person business, it doesn't matter how many more than one there are. The minute there is more than one, the whole dynamic changes. I much prefer being a one-person business.

So, why does it take a year or so to become profitable? Because most one person businesses run in the red for that period of time before they make any profit.

This book is about you. It will guide you through the process of start-up, marketing, sales, operations, administration, and finance. Those, after startup, are the five components of any business, and you, the one-person business owner, will be doing all five of them, for at least the first few months (or years). If you are already in business then the sections after the startup section will be for you also.

There will be two kinds of information in this book. First will be explanations of each of the five components. Secondly, there are many tip sheets to guide you through the processes in each component. These are in the Appendix section at the back of the book. They are there for you to think about, study, and practice.

I have chosen this format because it lends itself to easy, immediate use of the ideas. I have kept it simple, so you do not get into overwhelm and make mistakes. There is not a lot of frill and fluff and repetition in this book.

Small business is not rocket science. However, after reading this book you will see how much there is to think about and do. It can be overwhelming at times. So, relax, and enjoy the ride. Take it one step at a time.

I have included many mistakes and traps made by those who have gone before, so you do not have to repeat the mistakes or fall into the traps. If you take them to heart you will have a much easier time owning, managing, and working in and on your business. The mistakes and traps are in Appendix C, D, E, and F at the back.

It takes three things to be successful in small business. I call them the three D's. The first is Desire; you have to have some passion for your business. The second D is for Determination; you have to stick to it, be persistent; this takes will power. The third D is for Discipline; you have to really stay focused, and not let other things distract you.

If you have a sufficient amount of each of those D's, you stand a great chance of being successful. However, it also takes enough money. Not necessarily a lot of money, since some businesses can be started for hundreds, not thousands or tens of thousands of dollars. It takes whatever it takes, and you have to have that much. (See Appendix I for startup costs)

Introduction

If you don't have enough of the three D's and/or you don't have enough money, then forget it. You will be wasting your time. There are ways to determine how much is enough; more on that later.

Another rule of thumb is the three R's. The first is Right Place. The location of your business makes a big difference, be it in your town or city, or online, or at home. The second R is for Right Time. Timing is critical. You are at an advantage if you enter the market at the right time in terms of industry trends and product awareness. The third R is for Right Product. Only your market research will let you know if your product/service (and your service is your product) is one that will be in demand.

To own a small business, to be an entrepreneur, is a good thing. You are making it possible for people's needs and desires to be fulfilled. You are keeping money locally in circulation, which benefits the community. You are taking a stand for the American way. You are providing for yourself and your family. All of these things are worthy of respect.

It's about taking a risk. Business is a risk. You have four options:

1. **Avoid the risk. Don't go into business**

2. **Minimize the risk. Make it be safe; do the market research**

3. **Transfer the risk. Buy good insurance**

4. **Live with it. Self-insure and pray**

5. **Think carefully about the first four**

Remember, there is risk and then there is risk. If you are a single man or woman, with no family to support, and a low personal overhead, that's one thing. If, for example, you are middle aged, have a family, and a wife that thinks your business idea is crazy, then the risk looks very different. Also, the

The One Person Business

risk is different depending on how much or little money it will take to start the business. The bottom line is this; don't risk more than you can afford to lose if it all goes down the drain.

I have separated the book into five sections that correspond to the five components of a small business. Think of the fingers on your hand. One of them is your thumb, and it is the most important digit on your hand. The five components start with marketing; it is the thumb of your business, because without it there will be no sales, no operations, nothing to administer, and no money to count.

For that reason, this book will place much emphasis on your marketing, and the other four components will follow automatically. You will not use every tip sheet right away, and that's okay since they will be there for your use as you start and grow your one-person business.

I wish you great success and my hope is that this book will contribute to it. Let's get started.

Making Your Decision

Is Small Business Ownership Right for You?

At this point you need to see if owning any small business is compatible with your personality. Here is an exercise you can do to help you determine whether or not you will be emotionally comfortable owning a small business.

Give each factor a score of 3 points if you are sure your answer is yes; 2 points if your answer is 'sort of'; 1 point if your answer is no. Be really honest with yourself as you do this exercise.

____Do you like to make important decisions?
____Do you like to get things done on time?
____Do you react well to changes?
____Do you have the will power to grind it out?
____Do you like to relate to people?
____Do you like to be competitive?
____Do you enjoy planning for things?
____Is your health good enough to do this?
____Are you o.k. with the idea of losing the money you invest in it?

____Is working hard and long hours something you can do?
____Are you confident about your ability to do all of the five components; marketing, sales, operations, administration and finance?
____Do you like to take risks?
____Are you comfortable being in debt?
____Do you like to be busy?
____Do you enjoy thinking about business problems?

If your total score is 34 to 42 you are in good shape to do this.
If your total score is 22 to 33, maybe, maybe not.
If you total score is less than 22, probably this is not for you.

Start One or Buy an Existing Business or a Franchise?

The first question anyone thinking about going into business is this; should I start from scratch, or should I buy an existing business, or should I buy a franchise? There are advantages and drawbacks to each scenario. This book is mostly about starting from scratch, but if you are thinking about buying an existing business, see Appendix A in the back of the book. If you are thinking about buying a franchise business, see Appendix B in the back.

If you already have a business then read this book and use it.

Is Your Business Idea Viable?

First of all, does it satisfy the three R's, Right Place, Right Time, Right Product/Service? To be viable a business idea has to satisfy certain criteria.

____Is there enough of market for your product/service for you to sell enough to make the amount of money you need to draw from the business?

Making Your Decision

____Does your business idea mesh with your personal moral compass and ethics?

____Can you list at least three benefits your product/service will provide to your customers?

____Do you have any experience owning a business, or in the industry in which this business would be?

____Do you have enough money to start it, carry it until it is making a profit, and have a fund for unexpected expenses?

____Have you done any industry research to determine how much a business like this would make?

____Have you figured out the demographics of who your potential customer would be?

____Are legal considerations addressed in starting this business?

____Can you start it part time and keep that day job?

____How much knowledge does it take to run it?

____How much will have to be learned?

____How steep in the learning curve?

____Is this a dream or a potential nightmare?

____ Has it been done before; why not?

____Will it take more time and energy than it is worth?

____Will it wear you down quickly and cause burnout?

____Will it make enough money for you to justify the effort?

____What will be the profit margins? It is one thing to sell a lot of stuff; it is another to make a profit from it. Profit does not come from sales. It comes from what's left over after expenses and taxes. What are the financial margins going to be? If the gross and net margins are too low you will be fighting an uphill battle all the time.

____ Will it have repeat business? Repeat business means lower marketing costs. It is lots easier to find a new product or service to provide for a customer than it is to find a new customer. It's good if a product or service gets used up quickly, so they need to buy more.

A business idea is viable if, and only if, you can eventually answer yes to each of them. Remember, it is better to not do a business than it is to do it and have it fail. If you are not sure about this, see Appendix G.

12 Ways to See If Your Idea for a Small Business Fits You.

Is it your passion? Does it fit your lifestyle? Here are 12 ways to view it.

Rate these indicators YES or NO. Then you'll see how your business idea fits with you as a person.

❏ Yes, I have been involved with this product-industry-service before
❏ No

❏ Yes, I think about this a lot ❏ No

❏ Yes, I love to talk about it with friends ❏ No

❏ Yes, I love to talk about it with strangers ❏ No

❏ Yes, it would not seem like work to me to be doing it ❏ No

❏ Yes, I get very excited about being in <u>this</u> business ❏ No

❏ Yes, it fits my desire to work indoors or my desire to work outdoors
❏ No

❏ Yes, it fits my desire to work with people or to work by myself ❏ No

❏ Yes, it fits my desire to work in the daytime or nighttime ❏ No

Making Your Decision

❏ Yes, it fits my desire to be physically active or physically inactive
❏ No

❏ Yes, it fits my desire to deal with little details or my desire not to deal with them ❏ No

❏ Yes, it fits with my age and my gender ❏ No

The more YES responses the more likely you will be to personally fit with the business; the more likely you'll be to hang in there when things get tough (and they will at times); the more likely you'll be to stick to it and not get burned out quickly, and most importantly, you will psychologically enjoy doing it.

If you racked up a bunch of NO responses, perhaps that business is not for you.

Here are Seven Steps to Small Business Success.

1. **Plan properly.** Have a marketing plan, and a business plan, and a plan for growth (strategic plan).

2. **Monitor your financial data.** Generate an income statement and a balance sheet monthly, or at least every quarter. From these calculate your ratios. Then, analyze the ratios to see trends in your business; then compare the ratios with industry standards.

3. **Key Relationships;** Understand and analyze the relationship between your price(s), your cost(s), and your sales volume. Make any needed adjustments.

4. **Manage your cash flow.** Your bills have to be paid and you need to have the cash to pay them, and to avoid late fees and penalties. Create and maintain a cash flow chart.

5. **Manage your growth.** Create a strategic plan for where you want to go, how you plan to get there, what it will take in terms of capital, your labor, materials, marketing, etc. to get there.

6. **Borrow properly.** Be clear as to how much you need and how you will use the money. Do not borrow too soon or wait too late. Every successful business has debt - not too much and not too little. (See your ratios)

7. **Plan for Transition.** The time will come when you want to quit the business or sell the business. This needs to be planned for in advance.

10 Most Common Mistakes Made by Startup Owners

1. **Computeritis.** Either relying on them too much (being in love with them) or not enough (fearing them).

2. **Planning to give too much financial credit to customers.** You need cash.

3. **Renting too big an office.** It may be cheaper to relocate later. Image is not everything, even though it's important.

Making Your Decision

4. **Not having enough money.** It always takes more than you think it will.

5. **Overestimating sales.** Let yourself be surprised by underestimating them a bit.

6. **Choosing the wrong location.** Pay careful attention to this. (more on this later)

7. **Relying on one big customer.** This will cause you to not market enough.

8. **Ego. Not getting support and expert help when and if you need it.** Help is free and confidential at your local Small Business Development Center (SBDC). Check it out online at VASBDC.org.

9. **Not enough security.** Not enough protection and safety for your money and people.

10. **Not having a business plan** (see Appendix P)

Here are 16 More Common Mistakes Made by Startup Owners

1. **Using the wrong business name**

Don't keep the old name, if you bought an existing business, if the goodwill was overestimated. Don't create a new name if the goodwill was accurate or underestimated. Make your company name have marketing value. Do some market research to see if your potential customers like your new name before you change it. If most of them like it, use it, even if you don't like it, but not if you hate it.

2. Not Getting the Right Help

There is nothing wrong with needing help. All business owners need it at times. See yourself as a learner, rather than as a doer. You need to learn how to build the business, not just learn how to operate it. If all you do is operate it, you will not achieve your goals.

People you ask for help will be happy to help you. It makes them feel good about themselves. When you feel a need for help, get it right away. Time works against you if you don't. A good place to get it is at your local Small Business Development Center (SBDC) office.

3. Not Knowing Your Target Market

How to market is one issue. So is when to market. Where to market is just as important.

You cannot market to everybody. There is no everybody. That's just advertising, which is only one small part of marketing. If you don't know the age, sex, education level, occupational profile, and income level of your potential customer you are wasting your marketing money.

Why? Because you can't make the right promise of a benefit to them if you don't know who they are and what they want-need-desire.

4. Under-capitalization

This will happen if you: a. overestimate the sales revenues b. underestimate how much money you need to operate for the first year c. underestimate the budgeted overhead expenses d. underestimate the cost of the goods/services you will sell. This means that your projections* must be as accurate as possible and conservative.

You should try to arrange for additional capital for later before your business starts operating.

Making Your Decision

Even a business you buy could cause this if sales fall-off due to change of ownership; or sales may rise and you need more capital to handle the growth; or a change of suppliers could raise your cost of goods sold.

5. Wrong Form of Legal Structure

Any form is the right one, be it a sole proprietorship, an LLC, or P, S, or C corporation-but not for everyone at the same time. It depends on your situation. As a rule of thumb, start as a sole proprietor. You can easily shift to one of the others later, but it is hard to go the other way. For an LLC you can go online and do it yourself, or go to Legal Zoom.com or your own attorney. The decision should be based on how much risk there is that you may get sued, combined with how many valuable assets you might lose if you lost a law suit and you were a sole proprietor, like your house or cars.

6. No Business Plan

Why have one? It gives you better ability to project your sales, budgets, and cash flow. It is needed to get money from a bank or smart relative. It lets your suppliers know that you are financially sound and that you know what you are doing.

A business plan makes you think through all of the aspects of your business before you start operating. It substitutes a plan for plain old hope. (see Appendix P)

7. Wrong Location

Unless you are operating from your home, this is a very important decision. Maybe even the most important. (see Appendix H)

Here are some mistakes you could make: a. locate it where it is good for you, but not your customers or suppliers; b. locate it where it attracts a customer base that is different from the market into which you sell; c. misjudge how fast your business will expand and outgrow it too soon; d. locate where the lease is good for the landlord but not for you.

8. Not having good financial records

It's easy to have this happen. You open for business, the customers come, the money flows in, and you are too busy with the operations to do the deskwork. You can't manage well what you don't control. You don't control what you don't record. You can't analyze what you don't record. You can't make good decisions without good analysis. You can't compare income, inventory, marketing, etc., if you don't track it and record it.

You need to compare month by month, quarter by quarter, and year by year. You need a Profit and Loss Statement, a Balance Sheet, and some kind of Cash Flow Chart.

9. Not knowing how to price your goods or services.

Pricing is part of your marketing strategy. Just copying the competition is not the way to do it. You can't ignore what the competition is charging, but you must consider other important factors, or else your competition is pricing your product or service. What it costs you to sell your-product is not the same as what you paid for it from your supplier (if it's a tangible product). If it's a service, it's not just what you charge per hour for your service. Other factors enter in, like: a. your marketing strategy; b. how new your business is; c. your positioning in the marketplace. Sometimes price is not a big factor, depending on the niche you have or the demographic profile of your target market.

10. Not knowing how to hire. (There may come a time when you want to or need to)

To hire poorly will cost you more, in the long run, to rehire and then train a new person. You need to have the following to do it well: a. a written interview process b. a written interview questionnaire c. a written description of what the position tasks are, what the responsibilities are, and what the standards are by which it will be measured.

Making Your Decision

11. Not having a written agreement

No matter who it is with, even your spouse, put it in writing. Who is going to do what? Who will have authority to do what? What happens if one party violates the agreement?

12. Not marketing enough

Without marketing there will be no sales, no operations, no finances, and no business to own. Customers must be replaced on a regular basis. Nothing "sells itself". A business that is "well known" can also be forgotten. Customers die, leave town, saturate their need, go to your competitor, etc.

13. Not publicizing enough

If you don't tell your story, who will? People want and need to know the things that are unique about your company. Getting good publicity will magnify the value and the power of your marketing and advertising. "Name recognition" is more than half the battle.

14. Throwing money at problems

Money does not solve all problems. Putting more money into it may prevent you from taking a long hard look at what the problem really is.

Do not go out and borrow money to pour into your business unless you absolutely have to, since it may cause your business to go out of business.

15. Failure to outsource

You need to learn to let go. To outsource some functions of your business, as soon as you can, is the key to building a business and seeing it grow. If you can't emotionally afford to outsource, then don't go into business. To try to do it all yourself forever, and carry it all yourself, is not wisdom, it's folly. (There are exceptions, and you may remain a one-person business forever, but you can still outsource certain functions of your business).

16. Being too tied to the way it is

Nothing out there ever stays the same. Neither does a business. You must move with the changes or you'll lose touch with the business. Always staying in your comfort zone will keep you from the taking the necessary risks that are part of any business that is growing. "Change is good" should be your motto.

4 Risk Factors to Consider

Here are some questions you need to ask yourself *before* you decide to start or buy any business.

- **#1. Will I be the first to start this type of business?** If so, the risk is much higher. You need to test it more upfront, do more research upfront, and keep your day job for awhile.

- **#2. Is this business very cash intensive to begin?** Since most business run at a loss for a while after they start up, can you afford to wait until it becomes profitable? (1 year is average; some take 2 or 3 years to become profitable.)

- **#3. What is the risk potential?** Why risk $100,000 to make $500 a year?

- **#4. What degree of emotional risk can I handle?** Am I a person who loves challenge? Am I a person who is a risk taker? If I fail will it destroy me emotionally? Who besides me will it disappoint if the business fails?

All four of those questions are interrelated. If the money factor isn't right, there will be lots of hassle because of that. If the risk is too high for you, that will impact the money factor. If the marketplace is not as strong as it might be, both the money and the hassle factors will be impacted.

No one factor stands alone. A small business is a combination of all four factors, interacting with each other. Why risk it if it's too much hassle? Why hassle it if it's a poor marketplace? Why put your money in it if the risk is too high or the hassle too great?

Dealing With Your Fears.

We all experience it at times. Here is a list of the six most common fears of new small business owners. Which of these are you dealing with already?

Fear #1 - I'm afraid to fail; if it doesn't succeed, I'll be emotionally destroyed.

This can lead to a fear of making a total commitment to getting your business going. It has to be balanced against becoming a workaholic. However, loving your business a lot, putting your heart and soul into it is good. If it fails, and it might, as long as you have given your best effort then your business failed, but you didn't.

Fear #2 - I am afraid to let them see how scared I am.

If I let my guard down and admit to those around me in my family and friends that I'm scared and confused, then they will think less of me as a person. If you let them see the real you, fears and all, they will love you more for sharing the real you with them.

Fear #3 - If I make changes they won't work out.

If you don't make the changes that are needed it will come back and bite you in the rear later anyway. Your competition is constantly adjusting, changing things, trying new ideas. You will not succeed if you don't also do so.

Fear #4 - I'm afraid to risk it.

Life involves risk. Business involves risk. There is always some fear, but if it paralyses you into inaction then your business will suffer greatly. You have to make a distinction between manageable risk and foolhardy risk. But, some risk is necessary.

Fear #5 - I'm afraid to contact my present or past customers.

Back-end marketing is always a good idea. Those people might not accept your marketing offer, but they'll forget about you if you don't contact them, and that is also a form of rejection of them.

Fear #6 - I'm afraid to look at the numbers. Remember, business is about money-and money is about numbers.

You can put your head in the sand, but your business will get out of your control. Unless you pay attention to the crucial financial reports and marketing reports, and sales reports, and production reports, the fear you have of failing will turn into a reality. This is the moment of truth, and like the matador in the ring, you have to muster the courage. There is no way out of this.

We all experience fear at times. Owning a small business can bring fear up really quickly. When it rises, here are some tips on dealing with the fear.

See the fear as not being part of yourself. It's something you experience; it's not you. It's like food in your belly. It's in you, but it's not you.

Look at the fear as if it is an object, a thing, an entity. Decide whether you want the fear to increase, stay as it is, or go away. This is a conscious choice you can make. It's your fear, and you can decide to manage it rather than letting it manage you.

Talk to the fear as if it is a person. Tell it that it has no power (hey, it only has the power you give it). Don't tell it to go away. It won't listen. Tell it that it has no more power.

Talk to it as if it is a friend, not as an enemy. If you treat it as an enemy you are feeding it more energy. Don't resist it. Embrace it, then manage the fear.

Tell it, as a friend, that you are withdrawing the power you gave it. Remind yourself that it only has the power that you gave it, and you have every right to withdraw that power, since you gave it to it to begin with.

What is scaring you is not the problem. Giving your power to it is the problem. You can deal with that, and when you do it will empower you.

Making Your Decision

Here are Seven Keys to Small Business Success.

<u>Strategy</u>

Unless you think things out in advance and plan what you're going to do in both the short and long run you'll always be shooting from the hip. Not good.

<u>Risk</u>

Unless you can take a chance and get out of your comfort zone and try some new things you'll be repeating the same old mistakes over and over. Not good.

<u>Action</u>

Unless you move on it, and don't just sit around and think about doing it, nothing will get done. Not good. Move from Idea to Plan to Action.

<u>Priorities</u>

If everything is equally important, the really important things will not get done in a timely manner. Not good.

<u>Flexibility</u>

Things happen that you can't foresee. Unless you are willing and able to respond to them by considering other ways and means you'll use your old, inappropriate responses to the new problem. Not good.

<u>Goals</u>

Unless you know where you want to go how can you get there? Unless you have a view of the goal(s) you'll lose some of your focus and intention. Not good.

Reality

If you are not able to stay away from denial, and you hang out in fantasyland, you'll continually be making unrealistic decisions. Not good.

So, before we get into the five components, I want to share with you a list of the many mistakes and traps others have made and fallen into. You can then benefit from their mistakes and avoid making them (see Appendices C, D, E, and F).

11 Negotiation Tips

1. Remember, 'anything goes', so it's whatever a willing buyer and a willing seller agree on.

2. There are no laws to protect you in the negotiations

3. You are free to make a bad deal

4. Do not let the other party's anger distract you; it's a tactic he/she may use

5. Do not let the other side, if there are two of them, play good guy/bad guy

6. Do not make a concession without getting one from the other side

7. Remember, everything is negotiable

8. When one item changes, all other terms and conditions are then renegotiable.

Making Your Decision

9. **Be sure you set the time and place and rules for the negotiations**

10. **Remember, it is better to lose the deal than to lose your shirt**

11. **Do not let the other side rush you; stick to your own timetable.**

How to Legitimize Your Business

There are some simple steps to accomplish to make your business legal. Here they are:

1. **Register the name of your business.** This is called your DBA, also called your fictitious business name. This is done at your county government offices. It lets you know if you can use that name, and it prevents anyone else from using it in your county. It does not trademark the name; that is a whole different thing.

2. **Get the approval of the zoning office.** This is done at the city/county offices. Some businesses are not allowed in some locations.

3. **Get a business license.** The first year it is either free or a minimum charge. After that, it is based on your sales revenues. Some towns/cities do not issue a business license, so then you go to the county offices to get it.

4. **Get the estimated tax forms you will need to file each quarter.** You will need forms from both the IRS and your state. They are called the Estimated Income Tax Form. You have to call the IRS and your state offices to get the forms the first time. After that they mail them to you automatically each year.

5. **If you sell a product you will need to get a Resale Number from the jurisdiction that collects sales taxes.** This is usually the county they are paid to, but could also be your town or city. The resale number lets you avoid paying sales tax when you buy your materials or products. Your customer will pay the sales tax at the point of purchase.

Setting Your Business Goals

How can you get to where you want to go if you don't know where you're going? The way to know where you're going is to set a goal or goals.

Here are some tips:

1. **Be realistic.** Setting a goal that is not even remotely achievable is to set yourself up for disappointment. If the goal is achievable you at least have a chance of reaching it.

2. **Make sure that the goal is not subjective.** Be sure that it can be quantified in measurable terms. This allows you to compare the results with the goals and to keep track of progress toward the goal as you go along. Express the goal in specifics. It may be any type of goal, but it can still be stated in a clear and specific manner. Give it steps along the way.

3. **Give it a deadline.** Put in time steps along the way.

4. **Create a concrete plan for achieving the goal.** Map out what you will do, when you will do it, how you will do it, who will do it, etc.

5. **Celebrate the achievement of the goal in a positive manner.** Even if you are the only one responsible for achieving the goal, give yourself a celebration or reward.

Making Your Decision

6. **Not making the goal is not a failure; it's a challenge to do better next time.**

An interesting acronym for goals is this: SMART, which stands for <u>S</u>pecific-<u>M</u>easureable-<u>A</u>ttainable-<u>R</u>ealistic-<u>T</u>imely. Check on your progress toward the goal weekly.

Owning and running a small business, especially a one person business, is not a cake-walk. There are traps you can fall into. Take a look at Appendix F to see what they are.

To-Do List for Startups (Not every item will apply to you, but most will)

These are not in random order, but you do not have to go down the list item by item.

_____See if your idea for your business is really a good idea or not; is it viable?

_____Select a name for your business.

_____Register your fictitious business name (DBA) with your county.

_____Get a business license from the city or country in which you will do business.

_____Create your marketing plan. (see Appendix J)

_____Create your business plan. (see Appendix P)

_____Phone the state office or go on the web and sign up for a sales tax number.

_____Call the phone company and arrange for phone service.

_____Select the form of business entity you will use: sole proprietor or LLC; if not sure, consult a business attorney.

_____Get your graphics designed and ordered-business cards, signs, letterhead, brochure, web site, etc.

The One Person Business

_____Get a web domain address if you will need one and/or an e-mail address.

_____Pick a target date on which you will open for business (not too soon - it always takes longer than you think it will).

_____Select your business location (store front, office, warehouse, etc) and try to tie-it-up with a deposit without being totally committed.

_____Open a business checking account and business savings account in the name of your business.

_____Get your money together, both on-hand and available if needed.

_____If you need to make repairs or up-grades to your location, figure out what you need to do to it, the cost (get 3 bids), decide who to use.

_____Select the furniture and fixtures you will need.

_____Figure out which office machines and equipment you will need, cost it out, and set aside the money with which to buy them.

_____Figure out which business forms you will need and get them printed (order forms, receipt forms, contract forms, etc.)

_____Get the insurance you will need for your business. Buy only what you really need right now, but buy enough. One lawsuit could put you out of business.

_____Get a bookkeeping or accounting company to set up your business books if you don't know how, unless you are using a computer program like QuickBooks to keep your books.

_____Get sets of keys made for your new store/office/warehouse.

The Money to Start It

I am putting this section here, instead of in the finance component, because unless you understand this now, there is no point in your going any further. Remember, business is about money.

Making Your Decision

The Kinds of Money to Start It

First: Money for Startup Costs

You will need to buy things (machines, furniture, fixtures, supplies, etc.) pay for things (fees, licenses, permits, remodeling, signs, printing, rent deposit, etc. (See Appendix I for a pretty complete list)

Second: Money to operate it

You have to pay the bills that come in for materials, supplies, expenses, outsourced tasks, inventory, professional services, etc.

Third: Back-up Money

You will need a reserve fund to use if mistakes have been made in your sales projections, marketing projections, budgeting, etc. Bad News: You need all three of these before you start. Less than enough is not enough.

3 Sources

First: You get it from yourself (it is not advised to put it on your credit cards) and/or your circle of friends or relatives.

There are many sources in your personal life: savings; equity in your home; bank line of credit, loan from a relative; loan from a friend; taking a partner; life insurance policy; credit cards (not advised-the interest rate is too high). This is how almost all new businesses are started.

Second: You get it from outside yourself or your circle.

You get it from a bank loan, an Federal SBA loan or loan guarantee, a Virginia loan or loan guarantee, a venture capitalist. This is not how most startups get the money. Very few qualify to get it. If it is an existing business and you can borrow against assets or you have stocks and bonds or real estate to put up as collateral it may be possible, but it is not likely. Institutional lenders have at least six criteria:

The One Person Business

1. Really clean credit history, and no bankruptcies ever.

2. You have to work in the business, running it.

3. Your own initial investment (collateral) must be at least 30% of what you want to borrow.

4. You have to personally guarantee the loan and pay if back even if the business fails.

5. You have to have really good collateral with which to guarantee the loan. (see #3 above)

6. The business has to qualify with enough cash flow.

7. The business must have a debt to net worth ratio that meets guidelines.

<u>Third: Fantasy money</u>

You win the lottery; an angel comes out of nowhere and takes a liking to you and loans you the money; a rich uncle dies and leaves it to you in his will; the Wells Fargo truck crashes and a big bag of money rolls to your feet; you get picked to be on *So You Want to Be a Millionaire* and you win. Don't count on it.

If you don't plan for having enough capital (all three kinds) to start your business you could be out of business really fast.

Remember, start-up capital is of three kinds:

1. Money need prior to starting operations

2. Money needed to run it until you turn a profit

Making Your Decision

3. **Money in reserve to take care of mistakes in projections and budgets**

Here are the steps:
Calculate your "one time" start-up costs. This would be such things as lease/rent deposit; improvements to the office/building; signs, insurance, inventory, fixtures, permits, licenses, furniture, legal, etc. Call this figure A.

Then calculate your losses for the months you project that you will running at a loss. These numbers will come from your sales projections, budget projections, and Profit & Loss statement. Do not leave out the interest on any debts you have incurred to get started. What you are calculating here is the amount of the losses you will incur in the early months or years after start-up. Call this figure B.

Then calculate the <u>assets</u> you will be purchasing during the months you think you'll be running at a loss after you open. This would be things like equipment, more furniture, inventory, etc. Call this figure C.

Add the three, A, B, C together. This is the amount of working capital you will need. Now, figure out how much of a reserve you are going to put aside. Add this to the total of A, B, C. Call this grand total D.

If you use 25% of the total of A, B, C for your reserve you will probably be safe if you have a little experience in business. If you have a lot of experience you could probably use a lower percentage. If this is your first business, you might wish to use a higher percentage.

So, D is the amount of capital your business will need, no matter where it comes from, before you start operating.

If you don't have that much your risk of failure goes way up really fast. As you know, business is spelled bu$ine$$. Undercapitalization causes more businesses to fail than any other reason.

Projecting and Tracking the Money

There are three things to track (or do before you start) so you'll know where the money is coming from, where it is, where it went, and where it is owed.

<u>Sales Projections</u>

Before you even start your business and each month after you start you will need to make a guestimate as to how much money will come in from sales. This will help you regulate your spending, your borrowing, your buying, etc. This is not actually tracking it, it gets you ready to track it when it comes. (for details, see the Finance component)

<u>Budget Projections</u>

Before you even start your business and each month after that you will need to budget and adjust your budget. This is a guestimate as to how much you will spend on each budget line item. You can then compare it to how much you actually spent on each line item and make the proper adjustments. (for detail, see the Finance component; also you will find out about Cash Flow Projections there)

<u>Income Tracking</u>

At the end of each month you will need to create a Profit and Loss Statement. If you don't know how to do this, get QuickBooks or an accountant or bookkeeper. This will tell you how much money you made, how much you actually spent, and how much is left over as profit or not left over as a loss. To not do this is to commit business suicide.

<u>Net Worth Tracking</u>

At the end of each month you will need to create a Balance Sheet. This will tell you what the business owns (assets), what it owes (liabilities) and

Making Your Decision

what the difference is (net worth). The changes in these financial statements from month to month will help you manage the money in the business.

<u>Ratios</u>

Another way of tracking the finances is to analyze the business ratios. The data numbers come from the data on the Profit & Loss Statement and the Balance Sheet. They let you know how your business is doing from many different viewpoints. There are lots and lots of ratios to calculate, but in the early years of your business you will only need a few of therm. For more on ratios see Appendix N.

I assume you have read and digested all of the above helpful material. It is now time to get into the five components. Marketing is first because it drives the other four.

Marketing

The key to great marketing is to think about it from the perspective of your prospective customer. Get out of our own head. How will he or she react, relate, and respond to your marketing message. The message is just as important as the medium you use to deliver the message. Your marketing message has one purpose, which is to get them to call you/go to your website and buy. That's it.

Once they do that you are into sales, which also has only one purpose; to get the contract/order/cash money. Marketing and sales are not the same at all. They seem to be, like a horse and a zebra, but they are not. You will see that this is true after you read and digest both the marketing and sales components.

Another general principle of great marketing is that it must, I repeat, it *must* have an emotional impact on the prospect. People buy for a myriad of emotional reasons, and then they justify it in their minds. If your marketing message does not generate an emotional response, it will not produce the result you want. The material in this component is not in any particular order. You can skip around, come back, and use a particular item or not.

What you will have is a guide to planning your marketing so that it will produce the greatest result, lots of leads/customers. I include tips about retail, even though most retail businesses are not one-person businesses, but one could be. For example: a food truck, or a small volume electrician, or a handyman service.

Also, you should design your marketing as if you are speaking to one person, not to a group. Groups do not buy anything, only individuals do.

Remember, anything and everything can be part of your marketing, even including how you answer your phone, which should have a marketing aspect to it. For example, "Hello, this is Johnson Plumbing, where it's done right the first time. How may I help you?"

You must establish value in the mind of your prospective customer. People search for and buy value.

General Marketing Factors

Your Product/Service
    What benefits does it provide?
    How is it priced?
    What types/levels of service is customary?
    Where is it usually sold?
    Why do they buy it?
    What is the average sale amount?
    Who makes the buying decision?
    How many units are sold?
    Where do they make the buying decision?
    How do they finance the purchase?
    How is it packaged?
    How will it be used?
    How many are bought in a year?

The more of these you can find out about, the better your marketing will be. Industry trade associations are a good source of information.

Marketing

Creating Value

1. It is a feeling.

2. It is not a thing.

3. It is a relationship* between two things

4. It is what they buy

5. They feel that the benefits they expect to get are worth the value package**.

6. It is not just the money they will pay

7. If value is perceived to be there, price becomes less important

*Relationship

Quantity and Price
    Quantity and Quality
    Service and Quality
    Price and Quality
    Price and Quantity
    Quality and Obsolescence
    Price and Delivery time

**Value Package
    It is a combination of many factors:
    Tangible factors: Price, quality, quantity, delivery time, service

Intangible factors: status appeal, convenience, style, durability, etc.

From this point forward you will want your market research to guide you. There are many ways to gather the research data. Hire a marketing research firm. That's expensive. Contact /join the industry trade association. That's their business, to gather data.

Go see the local Small Business Development Center (SBDC); they will help you; their business advising is free and confidential.

Call or go see an owner of the same kind of business who is at least 100 miles away and take him/her to lunch and pick his/her brain.

Here are most of the things you want your market research to find out: (Nobody knows them all; you don't need to know every single one of them, but the more the better).

Demographics of Prospective Buyers:

In order to target your marketing you will need to know as much as possible about any and all prospective targets. This is called market demographics. Find out as much of this information as you can - the more, the better.

Age
Annual income
Male or female
Ethnicity
Occupation
Rent or own a home
When they buy
What they buy
How they buy
What they watch on TV
What books/magazines they read

14 Marketing Temptations to Avoid

#1 Temptation to copy your competitors

#2 Temptation to spend less than you need to

#3 Temptation to spend more on marketing than you need to

#4 Temptation to do too many things at once

#5 Temptation to put all your marketing eggs in one basket

#6 Temptation to do nothing

#7 Temptation to play stop and go marketing

#8 Temptation to sell-sell-sell and ignore marketing

#9 Temptation to transfer one factor to the other factors

#10 Temptation to just run an ad and be done with it

#11 Temptation to shoot from the hip without analyzing and tracking

#12 Temptation to do a "no brainer" and not check copy; and check it again and again

#13 Temptation to do too much, create so many sales that you can't fulfill them

#14 Temptation to "wing it" and not have a marketing system

Your Marketing Strategy

The first step in creating your marketing is to formulate a marketing strategy. This is your overall general marketing plan.

Do Not:
>Leave it to luck
>Leave it to chance

Do
>Create a plan
>Make it happen
>Stick to it, be fully committed to it, until and unless you decide to change it
>Double check the assumptions on which it is based

What a marketing strategy is Not
>A schedule of ads
>A series of sales letters or flyers, or whatever
>Any single thing
>A copy of what your competition is doing

A real marketing strategy Is:
>A game plan
>Based on a promise to your prospects
>Consistent with your company mission
>Consistent with your market niche
>Ties in with your company's uniqueness
>General to start with, and then gets more detailed as it does down the level of abstraction
>To position your company in the marketplace, not just your product
>Attentive to what the competition is doing or not doing in response to it
>Measured only by the results it creates

Marketing

It should attend to and include the following:
How you tell them; What medium(s) will you use;
What you tell them; What message do you want them to get?
Timing Spend your marketing budget all at once for a big entry, or a little at a time over time? When you do it is often more important than what you do.

Deciding what you can do (afford to do, have time to do, have staff to do) and what you can't do.

Deciding what you can say and what you can't say

Creating a time-line for the entire strategy

Creating a budget for the entire strategy

Creating due-dates for each part of it

<u>Plan it Organize it Develop it Implement it Track it Correct it</u> Take corrected action

After you have created your marketing strategy you then are ready to, and need to create your marketing plan.

Your Marketing Plan

To develop your plan you will skip around, do one part, jump to another part. In the end you will end up with a good plan. It is all about how you will implement your marketing strategy. See creating it as a problem solving process. Try to keep it simple and free of too much detail.

Here are the components of a good marketing plan: (more detail see Appendix K)

1. My primary marketing target is…

2. My market niche is…

3. The benefits I sell are…

4. I position my company by…

5. I will reach my prospects by…

6. My pricing strategy is…

7. I promote my business by…

8. My marketing budget is…

9. My marketing calendar is…

10. I will test and track these factors…

11. My marketing calendar will be…

Another way to approach your marketing plan is to focus on the five key parts. These key parts of marketing mix are:

Product/Service
Perceived value in the mind of the prospective buyer
New product or old
New industry or old
Benefits of it to the prospective customer
Features of the product
Guaranties/warranties

Marketing

Price
To the end user - how was it arrived at?
To the distributor or to another business
How is your price perceived?
Will it help you penetrate the market?
How sensitive to price and price changes is the market?
Discounts and allowances

Place
Location - Signage - Mail order - Web order - Telemarketing

Promotions
Advertizing Website Trade show Special sale Discounts Sales letter Personal selling Circulars Brochures Flyers

Packaging
Graphics - Size – Message on it – Materials – Durability - Aesthetics

Not every aspect of each of the four parts of the mix will apply to your business. That's all right, but be sure to cover all of the ones that do apply.

When you make a stew you have to put all of the ingredients in it in the proper mixture. It's the same with marketing. Having good ingredients is very important. So is how they are mixed together. Each part of it must be consistent with the other parts.

People
This is about demographics. What are the characteristics of your primary and secondary market targets? You cannot market to everybody; so,

which people will you market to? If you do not zero in on this you will be throwing your marketing dollars down the drain.

"Who you gonna' sell it to?" "To whom do you wish to sell it?" Either way, it's your target.

A market target is not the same as a market niche. They are related, but have slightly different functions.

Your target must be the following:

1. **Well defined Vague=no results.**

2. **Large enough If it's too small it's not worth targeting it**

3. **Reachable If you can't get your message to it for a reasonable cost, forget it**

Here are the steps:

1. **Pick your target <u>based on market research of demographics</u>**

2. **Decide how you will reach them**

3. **Decide why you will reach them**

4. **Decide when you will reach them**

5. **Decide what you will tell them**

What Do You Really Sell?

You may think you're selling bonds or plumbing or homes or hamburgers. But if your answer involves mentioning your product's features, you

Marketing

don't know what you're really selling! What you think you sell is not what your prospects and customers buy. If you think they buy a product or a service, think again.

Razor makers know that they don't sell blades. They sell comfort. Cosmetic makers know they don't sell lipstick. They sell romance.

Every product or service has at least one powerful motivator which can be used to seduce buyers into parting with their money in return for the promise of satisfaction. From lawnmowers to banks, if you know what you're really selling, and know how to promise the right satisfactions, you will do well. BUT – your Marketing Plan can only succeed if you identify your customers' inner motivations and the exact way your product can satisfy them.

Here is a list of what they really buy:

status, to impress others
benefits, not features
comfort, to reduce stress value, which is whether it is worth what they pay for it, in tangibles and intangibles, which are just as real as tangibles

freedom, to reduce or eliminate risk
solutions to their problems and frustrations
convenience, to take the hassle out of it
reputation, because they think positively about your company
selection, to have a greater number of things to choose from
promises, since they trust you will keep them
So, you should market one or more of these, not your product/service.

Positioning in Your Marketplace

The purpose of creating a position in the marketplace is to let your prospects know why it is that your company is different than your competitors. It creates a perception in the mind of your prospect/customer.

You can position your product/company on the basis of:
Convenience Features Service Selection or Price

You have to create a perception in the mind of your prospect. Perhaps they have a problem, or a frustration and they want somebody to make it go away. Or perhaps they have a fear or an anxiety, and they want somebody to at least make it be less than it is, and hopefully go away. Perhaps they have a very strong desire to have a certain thing or service.

If they are going to pick you to buy from, you need to be positioned in their mind as being preferable to your competition, to have a competitive advantage (CA).

There are some steps to this:

1. What is your company slogan?

2. What product or service do you sell?

3. How can you reposition those, redefine them, so the perception of your company changes for the better?

4. What fear or anxiety or frustration or problem will your company help them get rid of?

5. What name can you give to this?

6. Now, write a paragraph that captures the above factors that explains it in easy to understand terms.

Reaching Your Target Market

The next thing to figure out is how you will reach your market target(s). Here are the five steps to figure it out.

Marketing

1. **Pick your target or targets.** This should be based on your market research of the demographics. Don't make your target too big or it will cost too much to reach it. Don't make it too small or you will not generate enough sales volume.

2. **Figure out how you want to reach them, based on the cost of doing so.** Will you email to them or phone them or send a flyer, or use rack cards, or run an ad, do direct mail, or what? (direct mail see Appendix J)

3. **Decide why you will need to reach them.** To announce your grand opening, or to announce a sale, or to do a survey, or to tell them about a new product, or what?

4. **Then, decide when you will reach your target.** Will it be a one-time thing, or once a week, or once a season, or what?

5. **Create your message.** Be sure to do a few versions and then pick the best one. Be brief, be consistent with your positioning, and tell them the benefits, not features or your product/service. Do not forget to put in a call to action, where you tell them what you want them to do-call, come in, go to website, whatever.

Now it is time to calculate how much of a total market share you want/need to capture. It is the percentage of the total market into which you sell that you want to capture. Here is how to calculate it.

Method #1 Average Competitor Sales
Retail Sales ÷ No. of Competitors = Average Sales per Business
Method #2 Average Customer Base
Market Population ÷ No. of Competitors = Average no. of people per competitor

Watch Out!

1. Do not overestimate your market share. Calculate it twice; once at what you expect, and once at close to your breakeven point.

2. Be sure you do not estimate at a number higher than your capacity to fulfill/service that number of orders.

3. Do not estimate your target market too broadly. See #2 again.

4. Be sure your target market is large enough to make you a profit.

74 Tips on Web Site Marketing & Social Media

It is now a truism that any business, every business, your business needs to have a website. Nearly everyone these days goes on the internet to find out about anything.

Here are 74 tips on how to construct your website, some tips about marketing on it, and tips on social media marketing. These tips will get you off to a good start. They are in random order. As you go through the tips, put a check mark on the ones you need to pay special attention to.

1. Offer only one service or product on your home page.

2. Do not spam if you use email marketing. Your site will be shut down.

3. Try to install a sense of a need for the prospect/customer to act NOW. One way is to give them a discount if they buy by a certain

Marketing

date. Another way is to tell them there are only a limited number left.

4. Use the words 'you' and 'your' a lot.

5. Use a little bit of bold and italics and highlighting.

6. Have your paragraphs be of varied lengths.

7. Put in sub-headlines where appropriate.

8. Do not justify the right hand edge of your page. Leave it uneven.

9. Bullets are good to use for emphasizing key points.

10. Change the headline every so often and test and track the results.

11. Keep the home page content all above the scroll line.

12. You must own the domain name.

13. Be sure your web host sets it up so that you own your website. If they own it, get them to waive, in writing, their ownership rights.

14. You must be able to change the website by yourself.

15. The home page must be clean, with lots of white space.

16. The home page should have a photo and perhaps a video embedded in it.

17. There must be tracking of analytics, especially the bounce rate, which should be under 30%.

18. It must be social media compatible and linkable to social media.

19. The colors must be consistent with the company graphics.

20. There must be link capability, but don't overuse links.

21. There should to be a QR code if you do retail.

22. The homepage should have a headline, one that asks the viewer a question and/or promises a benefit

23. The site has to contain meta tags, and many template sites do not

24. Since Google looks at the first 250 words of the content, put a keyword phrase in the content once or twice, not more. However, put all of your keyword phrases on your home page.

25. Put in a "trade", where you offer them a free something, in exchange for their name, their email address, their phone number, and a question or comment. The 'trade' can be anything they will appreciate and want to have. Examples: chance to enter a contest or free subscription to your newsletter or teaser portion of a handout or anything you can think of.

26. Do not use 'flash', as it will not show up on mobile sites.

27. Put at least one keyword per page after the home page.

Marketing

28. Make a short video, put it on YouTube and imbed it on your home page.

29. The phone number must be on every page.

30. The phone number must be 'text'

31. The web designer, if it's not you, should have 'E&O' insurance in case of a lawsuit.

32. Use power verbs, not adjectives.

33. The domain name should be keyword rich.

34. Maybe have two or three domain names that all feed to the home page or to a landing page.

35. What is the website about; what is the purpose? This should match your call to action.

36. Put a title on each page.

37. Use meta descriptions; a few sentences, not stuffed with key words, unique for each page; keep it simple.

38. The URL should have no capital letters, and should use relevant words.

39. Keep your content easy to read; put in key words in the content of each page; use heading tags, and don't forget to put in a call to action.

40. With links, keep anchor text short and descriptive; avoid CSS styling

41. With images, do not use an image for navigation

42. Make sure that GoogleBot-mobile can access the site

43. Make sure you know where your business is getting reviewed and monitor these sites regularly so you can respond when there is a new review. When there's a positive review, acknowledge it and say thank you. When there's a negative review, apologize and offer to make it right.

44. Add social media sharing buttons on every page.

45. Make sure that any and all of your social media marketing links to your website.

46. Take care when you or your web designer select the font(s) to use. This is more important than you may think. Do not use Times Roman.

47. Your website navigation bar should never ask the viewer to make more than 3 clicks to get to what they want to find on your site. Always use customer words, not industry jargon, on the buttons. Do not have too many options, too many buttons. Consolidate. Have only one navigation bar, probably horizontal at the top part of the home page.

48. Your navigation bar must have a home button, an 'about us' button, and a 'contact us' button, plus any other buttons you need.

Marketing

If you sell on the web, it must have a "shop now" button, using those two words.

49. Have lots of inbound links to your site.

Social Media Marketing

50. The purpose of business social media is to drive viewers to your website.

51. Facebook and Twitter are the best social media to begin with.

52. Blog posts can be drawings, photographs, opinions and gossip.

53. Any lead you get from any social media needs to be a qualified lead, which means they have given you their contact information.

54. Social media is not just for advertising your business. Give them something that they will find valuable.

55. If your website is for selling on the internet, do not try to sell anything that is too big to fit in a grocery store shopping cart.

56. Here is the path: social media»»your website»» leads»»sales.

57. For a Blog go to Got-Clicks.com to see a free tutorial on blogging.

58. Do not post when you are angry, been drinking, or at work.

59. Do not post too often.

60. Do not post raunchy photos.

61. Know the social media sites and how they work.

62. Choose your social media sites with care.

63. Who will manage your social media posting?

64. How will you track each social media you use to see if it is working?

65. How long will you wait to see if it is working?

66. How much time will you budget for doing social media? It takes time.

67. Have a clear goal for each type of social media you use.

68. You can be a guest blogger on other people's blogs.

69. Make a list of topics you will blog about.

70. Have someone else check it over before you send it out.

71. Try sending it out to as few people and get some feedback before sending it out in mass.

72. Put your blog on your website.

73. Each blog should have a specific theme.

74. Put pictures and/or a video on your blog.

Marketing

Creating Your Brand

You can and should use your brand image and values in many places: office décor, letterhead, website, packaging, on products, promotional materials, social media sites, business card, shirts, emails, etc.

1. Your company brand is intangible; it is a collection of thoughts and feelings; it is not a commodity, not a product.

2. The purpose is to create customer loyalty; this is built from consistency of experience of your potential/actual customer.

3. Brand is created from your company name, slogan, logo, symbols, characters, etc.

4. What is the personality of your company; if it was a person, how would he/she look, act, sound, present himself/herself? List a few adjectives that describe the person.

5. The intangibles must be perceived to be effective, otherwise it's just a commodity.

6. It is one unique idea, user focused, (or at most two); it is single-minded.

7. It must differentiate your company from the competition.

8. It is built over time, not in a day; it is built from exposure and experience.

9. It is based on the promise your company makes to the customer, your USP, which is your Unique Selling Proposition.

10. It is holistic, a collection of 'touch points' that connect with your customer.

11. The touch points need to be consistent, simple, meaningful, easy to recognize, usable in different mediums, and without any negative connotations.

12. The visual and verbal content must feed off of each other.

13. Make it appeal to specific demographics.

14. Use the active voice in written content, not the passive voice.

15. On the web, each page should have the same structure.

16. Put a photo on each posting to social media; up to 480 pixels X 480px

Your Image in the Marketplace

People have a perception of your business. Your customers do, your suppliers do, your creditors do. It is up to you, as part of your marketing, to make sure it's a positive perception.

Your business needs to make a good impression and keep on making it, to reinforce that first impression.

Here are seven things you need to pay attention to:

1. Visual package

Do your business cards, brochures, letterhead, stationery, order forms, invoices, signs, etc. all give the same impression? Are they in sync with each other, with colors, fonts, etc.

Marketing

2. Your Office

When customers, clients, suppliers, bankers, delivery persons come in does it look inviting; does it look neat and orderly; does it feel inviting. Is there good seating, good control of the temperature, etc.? Is there an absence of noise?

3. Your Telephone

Is it always answered by the third ring? Is there a smile in the voice of the person answering it? Does the answering machine sound like it's in a tunnel? If a caller is put on hold does he get attention every 60 seconds? Do you return calls no later than 24 hours after they come in? Do you get the caller's name, phone number, email address, and reason for calling from every call? That's the goal.

4. Your correspondence

Do your letters look like a professional secretary wrote them and typed them? Is the paper they are printed on good quality paper? Is the spelling absolutely accurate?

5. Your Professionalism

Do you avoid using slang and cuss words? Do you dress in a manner appropriate to your business? Does your staff wear shirts or uniforms with our company name or logo on them? Do you have all of the business machines you need to look like a business and not a hobby?

6. User-friendly

Are your office procedures, customer ordering procedures, shipping procedures easy for your customer and suppliers to understand and use (user friendly)? Do you make things convenient and time saving for them?

7. Follow-up

Do you make special effort to contact an unhappy customer? Do you call those to whom you owe money to assure them you will pay them soon? Do you remind those who owe you money in a businesslike manner?

Writing a Great Headline

This is important because your headline will either capture the viewer's attention or it won't. If it doesn't, then the rest of your marketing piece will not be read. All that time, energy, and money will be for nothing.

A headline can be used in many marketing places. Here is what it should do: (pick those that apply)

- **Offer a benefit**

- **Make a promise**

- **Identify the prospect**

- **Give news**

- **Identify a problem**

- **Make an offer**

- **Tell a story**

- **Be very clear**

- **Be specific**

- **Look good visually**

Marketing

No headline can do all of those at once. Your task is to get as many of them as you can into your headline.

<u>Key Questions:</u>
Does your headline communicate your message?
Does it talk to a specific target market?
Could a competitor put their name on it and run it? (not good)
<u>Uses for headlines</u>
Newspaper ads Brochures Radio spots Flyers Rack cards Door knockers Sales letters and on and on

Competitive Advantage (CA)

It is important to create for your business an advantage in the competition with your competitors. Here are some tips.

1. Don't be afraid to be different Be unique, then use it.

2. Figure out why people choose you over the competition-then market that.

3. Your competitive advantage must be sustainable; continue to be important to your customers.

4. Your CA should <u>not</u> be:

    Price (too easy to copy)
    Subjective (not "we give the best customer service")
    Arbitrary or a cliché

5. A CA can be internal; great training, great distribution, etc. or external-visible to the customers

6. You must play to win, not just participate in the marketplace

7. Always test the use of your CA to see if it will last a while

8. Your CA could be what nobody else does

9. It should be something others cannot easily copy

10. It should have potential to grow

11. It must have value to the prospect/customer/client, or forget it

12. It should be quantifiable to the prospect/customer/client

13. Use your CA in your slogan or packaging or website or social media, etc.

Words to Use/Not Use in Marketing

<u>Good Words</u>: free you your new fun gain love now introducing easy proven win proud benefit advantage money sale save results discover announcing value guaranteed security fee agreement

<u>Bad Words</u>: pay: price deal deposit cost buy contract sign obligation fail loss wrong order difficult hard

Graphic Design Factors

Graphics have a lot to do with your marketing. How it looks is often as important as what it says. Here are the five most important factors to consider when you do a business card, brochure, website page, flyer, etc.

Marketing

1. What is the main concept you're trying to communicate? It can be one word or a few words.

2. Keep it short and concise.

3. It has to be clear. This means it is easy to see and understand.

4. Make it original, be creative. Use shape, color, type font and size wisely. Try to avoid Times New Roman font.

5. Be consistent. All of your graphics should have the same visual message.

Your Logo

It is a symbolic representation of your company.

Put it on everything-your website, your business card, your brochures, your flyers, your signs, etc.

The purpose of your logo is to create 'top of mind awareness' of your company.

You can use words, or symbols, or both.

Keep any words short; keep any symbols very simple.

Keep colors consistent through your marketing, on your website, your business card, your brochures, your flyers, your signs, etc.

Use complimentary colors; go to Google 'color wheel' to pick them.

To find images, Google the type of business you have and then the word 'images'.

You can get a professional logo done for about $300 from 99designs.com They send out your idea to 100's of graphic designers, as a contest, and within one week you will have your logo. All of them submit a design and you pick the one you like. You can modify it, and you will own it. You will answer questions about what you want and they will work with your answers.

Naming Your Business

If you are just starting your business, or you need to change the name of a business you bought, here are some tips:

1. Can your company name be pronounced easily, even musically?

2. Can you say it without regularly being asked to spell it?

3. Does it read quickly and clearly-or does the reader have to pause to consider it?

4. Is it spelled as it sounds?

5. Is it short-eleven letters and 4 syllables maximum?

6. Does it look good when printed?

7. Does it "fit" with your company logo?

8. Is it unique or sensory, two traits that make words memorable?

9. Does it set the right tone?

10. Is it consistent with your marketing strategy with regard to: a. price. b. quality, c. time, d. selection, e. reliability

11. Is it different from your competitor's names?

12. Do a few people dislike it? (A good sign. Good names have edges)

13. Does it express or imply a desirable message, a benefit?

Marketing

Your Slogan (tag)

1. It should be 2 to 7 or 8 words. No more. The fewer, the better.

2. It should be easy to read, easy to say, and easy to remember.

3. It has to be authentic; it must reflect what you do and why you do it.

4. If they cannot remember it, it's no good.

5. It must be unique.

6. It should be timeless; it will not need to change all the time.

7. It can be a sentence, or a phrase, or words separated by dashes.

8. It must be consistent with the name of your business.

Examples: Only Vegas - Built Ford Tough - Eat Fresh -
The pause that refreshes - We are professional grade -
On time-Every time

Pricing

This is critical. Your pricing is a big factor in how you are perceived in the marketplace. If you price too low you run the risk of a perception of poor value or quality. If you price too high you lose potential customers. Remember, ineffective pricing strategies are one of the key causes of failures of small businesses.

You must price to cover direct costs of production, variable overhead, fixed overhead, owner wages (draw), and profit.

Kinds of Pricing Strategies

<u>Cost-based</u>

This is where you set the price high enough to cover COGS (cost of materials plus your labor) and all overhead operating expenses, and whatever profit percentage you wish to earn. This is often called mark-up pricing. The term 'keystone' refers to cost-based pricing where you simply double the cost you paid for it, and that is then your price.

<u>Psychological pricing</u>

In this strategy you set the price at a number that is psychologically more comfortable and attractive to the customer. For example, $39.95 instead of $40.00

<u>Decoy pricing</u>

In this case you raise the price on one item to make a lower price on a similar item more attractive.

<u>Competition-based pricing</u>

It is very common to set price at the same or near what the competition is charging. Be sure that you set it high enough to cover all costs. Also be sure that the competition is not way off in their own pricing.

<u>Up-Down pricing</u>

You can set your price higher than the competition and then offer discounts, coupons, promotions, etc. Offer it at both the higher price and the lower price.

<u>Market based pricing</u>

This is the price that the market will bear. It is based on the demand level for the product/service in relation to the supply of the product/service.

Marketing

Slow Times pricing

You drop the price because sales are slow, or due to seasonality, or you have a special sale going. Your margins will be smaller, but you will still stay in the black.

Market Share pricing

If you are just opening your business you may wish to drop prices so you can lure customers away from your competition.

Be aware that you can and may change your pricing strategy as things change in the marketplace. Prices should not be cast in stone.

When you check out what the competition is doing, here are a few things to check out: how many competitors are there; are they bigger, the same size, or smaller than you; what pricing strategies do they use?

Here are 11 tips about pricing:

1. Listen to your customers; they can guide you in your pricing.

2. Try to be flexible and open to changing your pricing as the situation changes.

3. Customers are more sensitive to prices if there are alternatives to what you sell.

4. Customers are less sensitive to prices if it is hard to compare your product/service to your competitors.

5. Higher price is often indicative of higher quality, and customers will pay more if they perceive it to be of higher quality.

6. Customers will not buy from you if they think your pricing is not fair or reasonable.

7. Bundling items into 'packages' makes them less price sensitive.

8. Be sure to track sales in relation to pricing. You may make more profit with a lower price or vice-versa. It's better to sell 10 at $2 each than to sell 5 and $3 each.

9. The best time to change pricing is just before Spring and just before Fall.

10. Be sure to pay attention to whether your pricing fits your market.

11. Since poor pricing is a major cause of business failure. Test it, track it.

This component on marketing ends on a subtle but important concept. <u>Customers do not buy the product/service you sell.</u> They buy some emotional benefit(s) they will get from it.

Sales

Selling is about listening. I'll say that again. Selling is about listening. When you sell the customer/prospect should do 80% of the talking and you do 20%. That's how you find out what you need to know to close the sale. What does he or she want; what does he or she need? What is his or her 'hot button'? What are his or her objections, considerations, stalls? To what point has your marketing brought the prospect?

Since you are a one-person business, you are the salesperson. When you get a prospective customer/client on the phone or in your store, or at the prospects site, or to your website if you sell on the web, then it is time to stop marketing and start selling.

It is a myth that sales people are born. They are trained, and this component will go a long ways to training you. Not all the way. Only experience and practice can do that.

There is only one goal. *Make the sale.* That's it. Everything else is a distraction on the path to closing the sale. Let's face it. If you don't close the sale there is no sale, no income, and no profit.

Sales Strategies

Any sales strategy might use more than one of these. No sales strategy would use all of them. Different types of products and services lend themselves to different strategies. Some of them cost more emotionally than others cost. Some of them are more reliant on personality. Use the ones that fit the situation and that work for you.

<u>Relationship Driven</u>

This is the traditional type. You rely on creating and maintaining a good personal relationship with the decision maker, and his staff, if any, and you massage that relationship continuously. You take the prospect to lunch, you send gifts, you send referrals, you call just to say hi and see how things are going, etc.

<u>Presentation Driven</u>

This type relies on the presentation itself to do the whole job. It puts on a "dog & pony" show in an attempt to "wow" the prospect into buying.

<u>Price Driven</u>

This places focus on how it will cost less than the rest, provides discounts of all kinds, gives away add-ons for free, meets and matches any competitors bid or price, gives coupons, etc.

<u>Pressure Driven</u>

This relies on frequency of calling, frequency of visiting, using a more aggressive style. If you never let up, it says, they will eventually capitulate and buy.

<u>Anxiety Driven</u>

This tries to scare them into being so afraid not to buy that they buy. It tells them about how prices are going to up soon, or how this item will be discontinued soon, or how there are only a few left, etc.

Pity Driven

This tries to create "feeling sorry for" the salesperson or company. We're the new guy on the block, or we're about to go under if we don't get sales, or it brings up a personal life problem to elicit sympathy.

Status Driven

This relies on testimonials by famous people, by stars, to endorse or recommend your company/product/service. It implies that the status of the endorser/recommender will rub off on the buyer.

Advertising Driven

This relies on continuous running of ads to keep the company name in front of the prospects. It hopes to keep the choice of company/product in the forefront of the mind of the prospect.

Your Sales Plan

A closed sale is not an event. It's the end result of a process. Like any complex activity it should be planned. There are many pieces to the sales plan puzzle. Obviously, not all apply to a particular sales situation. Get creative; pick what will work for your situation.

Telephone Cold Call
Return Phone Call
Follow-up Phone Call
Sales Presentation by Appointment (for 2 or 3 step process)
Sales Presentation by Drop-In
Solution Presentation (for 3 step process)
Sales Letter
Follow-up Letter
Price Quote
Mail materials

The One Person Business

After sale re-sell
Request for referral in person
Request for referral by mail
Survey/Questionnaire
Other _____
Other _____

Now, it's time to put the pieces of the puzzle together by arranging the items above in the order in which you will use them. <u>You will probably not use all of them.</u> After you have put them in order on a piece of scratch paper, Put the paper away and do it again an hour later. See if it comes out the same. Keep doing it until you are completely satisfied with the plan. Then, figure out what sales materials (brochure, business card, script, quote form, etc.) you will need for each piece of the plan.

Your Sales Process

Selling is that, a process. No one part or aspect of it is more important than another. The person doing the selling, and it is most likely going to be you, will need to have a plan, to establish rapport with the prospect, to make a presentation, and to close the sale. The two step or three step process are:

1. **Not for retail selling**

2. **Not for order taking where prospect calls you to place an order**

3. **Not for one-step selling**

<u>Two Step Process</u>

1. **Get the appointment**

Sales

You cold-call them, from a list or a referral

They call you in response to an ad, brochure, website, flyer, etc.

2. Make a sales presentation

<u>Three Step Process</u>

1. Get the appointment
You cold-call them, from a list or a referral
They call you in response to an ad, brochure, flyer, etc.

2. Discover what they need: product/service

3. Return to prospect to present your solution to his/her problem

<u>Tips for either 2-Step or 3-Step</u>

1. **Your sales process must be consistent with, and reinforce, your marketing positioning.**

2. **The sales process begins somewhere in your marketing process, not when you get in front of the prospect.**

3. **The sale does not end with a signature; many times reselling is needed. Buyer remorse is real. They can un-sell themselves as fast as you got them to sell it to themselves.**

4. **Your sales process should not look or sound like a sales process. You are there to help, advise, consult, explain, guide-but not to sell.**

5. Do not try to manipulate the buyer. He/she will check out and refuse to buy.

6. Sell value, not the product. Value is the relationship between one thing and another, like, for example, price and quality.

7. Each part of the sales process must create in the prospect a *feeling* of value.

8. The focus must be on the <u>prospect</u>; not on you; not on the product; not on your service or your company.

Step 1. Get the Appointment

- ☐ You must talk <u>with</u> them, not to them or at them.

- ☐ In retail, the appointment is getting them to talk with you. If they don't, you are not selling; you are just watching the store.

- ☐ Speak slowly and clearly.

- ☐ Keep it short and to the point.

- ☐ Focus on your one goal-to get the appointment-not to sell anything.

- ☐ Always speak from a prepared script that you have practiced and practiced.

- ☐ Remind the prospect of the benefits they will get

Sales

- ☐ Do not give up after an unsuccessful attempt. Call again and again.

- ☐ Be sure you are speaking to the decision-maker, or at least to the decision-influencer

- ☐ Getting past the "screener" secretary or clerk

    a. Be friendly, sincere, serious, and non-aggressive

    b. Make him/her feel important to the process

    c. Appeal to his/her self-interest. Offer a psychological gratification (how your product/service will provide benefits to the boss/company and make the screener look good) or provide for screener a relief from anxiety; use doubletalk* to confuse the screener so he/she will think, "I don't understand this, but it may be important."

    d. Offer a free gift to the boss. The screener will not want to be responsible for the screener not getting it.

    e. Tell him/her you're impressed by how well he/she takes care of the boss.

    f. Be creative; you never know, it might work.

    g. State the number of minutes you will need. Keep it low.

    h. Provide a choice of times for the appointment

i. Use phrases that imply or state a benefit

> Examples: "We've created a very creative way for you to deal with XXX and I'd like an opportunity to bring the benefits of it to you"
> "We've created a system that makes it possible for you to…"
> "We've found a remarkable way to provide a solution to a very real problem that I'm sure you've experienced in your job/business."

Step 2. Sales Presentation
1 If you are using a 2 step sales process, this is the last step and you must present and close at this step.

1. **Whether done in writing or verbally, always present it in person**

2. **The questions you will ask and the statements you will make should be scripted in advance.**

3. **At the start make some statements that let him/her know that you know what you're talking about**

4. **At the start get the prospects agreement as to how long it will take**

5. **Repeat, to reinforce it, what you said when you set up the appointment**

6. **Find out what it is in the prospect's job or company that is producing frustration, anxiety, or fear.**

7. Secure the prospect's willingness to do something about the cause of it.

8. Present your solution; explain the benefits; how will your product/service solve his problem?

9. Do a trial close

10. If positive, close. If negative, go back to step 2 and find the real problem.

Step 3. Solution Presentation

If you are using a 3 step sales process, omit steps 4, 5, and 6 from step 2. Then add these steps:

1. Make an appointment, with specific date, time, and place, for you to return to present your solution.

2. Go back to your office and put together you Solution Presentation; gather all of the facts, data, pricing, etc. that you will need when you return to the prospect.

3. Prepare the written agenda of your solution presentation.

4. Present your solution; explain the benefits; how will your product/service solve his problem?

5. Do a trial close

6. If positive, close. If negative, go back to step 2 and find the real problem.

Maxims, Tips and No No's

6 Sales Maxims

1. A sale is not about selling. It's about buying. What gets them to buy?

2. Selling is about making them feel that they are in control, when in fact you are.

3. Selling is about asking, about counseling, about advising; it's not about selling.

4. You don't sell anything; <u>the buyer must sell it to himself or herself.</u>

5. The sale is made in the first few seconds or minutes. It is impossible to have a second chance at a first impression.

6. Selling is about the buyer; it's not about you.

28 Street-Smart Sales Tips {not in order of importance}

1. Call-call-call those prospects and customers. Contact is the key to sales success.

2. Be available to them; they have questions, you have the answers.

3. Stay as positive in your attitude as you can.

4. Be as brave as you can; fear of failure can cause the failure.

5. Don't be afraid to be competitive; business is competitive.

6. Sell the appointment before you try to sell the product/service.

7. Sell the benefits first. Features come third, after you sell the value.

8. Closing is simply asking for the order; don't shy away from the asking.

9. How frequently you should call-visit-mail to the prospect/customer depends on the potential impact of each call-visit-mailer.

10. Your best prospect is always your existing or previous customer.

11. If your marketing positioning and sales strategy are consistent and coherent there is very little "selling" to be done.

12. Buying decisions are made emotionally and then rationalized in the mind.

13. Selling is about listening, not talking.

14. Being assertive is not the same as being aggressive.

15. Be there to serve, not to sell; this will allow you to remain emotionally uninvolved.

16. Never assume or try to read the mind of your prospect. Ask.

17. If the prospect/customer gets excited about it, don't join him in the excitement; ask him what has excited him, so then he sells it to himself.

18. Anticipate sales objections and diffuse them before they come up.

19. Buyers buy for their reasons, not yours.

20. Never apologize for price; justify it with value.

21. Have a prepared response for every objection you anticipate coming up.

22. Buyers buy what they want, not what they need.

23. A sales presentation should be an interview, not a speech.

24. Do not try to talk the prospect out of his fear; remove what is causing the fear.

25. Do not try to change the prospect's decision; give him new information so he can make a new decision.

26. You can't sell anybody anything; they have to discover that they want it. If they want it enough they will think they need it.

27. The sales process creates a perceived gap between where the prospect is and where s/he wants to be; this gap must be experienced emotionally, not just intellectually.

28. Focus on the emotional gratification the prospect will receive, not on the commodity or service you sell; avoid talking about your product until after the emotional commitment is made by the prospect.

Now, go back over the list and pick out the three that you think are the most important tips. Ask yourself why you feel each is so important. Do this again tomorrow and see if they are the same three

14 Sales No-No's Don't Do These Things in Sales

If you are in the habit of doing any of these, break the habit. If you do not do them, then never start to.

1. Never go to any sales presentation unprepared. Your chances of making the sale are nil.

2. Never take the first 'no' personally. You are being tested to see if you are serious.

3. Never think that the phone will ring with no effort from you. This is 'magical thinking'.

4. Never promise something you can't deliver. You'll lose all of your credibility.

5. Never assume that the prospect/customer can't afford it. Appearances may deceive you.

6. Never stop selling until the buyer has stopped buying. Go for add-ons, upgrades, etc.

7. Never apologize for the price. Justify it with value.

8. Never try to sell during a cold call. Get an appointment and sell then.

9. Never walk away without getting a referral. It's your next sale opportunity.

10. Never beat yourself up if things aren't going well. Work on getting better.

11. Work on improving your strengths; spend much less time working on improving your weaknesses.

12. Never accept "I'll think it over". Ask, "Please tell me why you decided not to buy."

13. Never fake an answer. Answer the question with a question. Use a 'softening statement' like "I'm glad you asked me that" or "That must be an important question to you"

14. Never box yourself into a corner. Ask; don't assume anything.

Body Language in Closing the Sale

80% of all human communication is non-verbal, mostly via body language. Pay attention to it, it will teach you a lot about your customer, client, prospect.

Sales

<u>Negative</u>

HANDS IN POCKET - Insecure; afraid of you; very defensive

FOLED ARMS - Too defensive; do not try to close at this time

LOOKS DOWN, FACE TURNED AWAY - Is not believing you. Do not try to close

RUBS NOSE - Thinks you're lying; do not try to close

PUTS HAND OR FINGERS OVER MOUTH - Watch it; he or she is probably lying to you

TAPPING OR DRUMMING FINGERS - Impatience; stop talking, go for the close

STROKING CHIN - Thinking about it; ask for signature; be quiet

STEEPLING FINGERS - He or she thinks they are smarter than you; do not try to close yet

RUBS BACK OF NECK - Does not agree with what you are saying

CONTRACTED EYE PUPILS Do not go for the close

PULLING AT EAR - Undecided; on the fence; continue selling

<u>Positive</u>

BITING NAILS - Nervous; be friendly; go for the close

The One Person Business

DILATED EYE PUPILS - Go for the close

HEAD TILTED TO SIDE - Very interested; go for the close

RESTS HEAD ON HAND - Paying attention to you; go for the close

PATS OR FONDLES HAIR - Go for the close

LIGHTS A CIGARETTE - Go for the close

Closing the Sale

1. There is no one "right" way. Each selling situation is unique.

2. The "close" can come at <u>any</u> point in your sales presentation.

3. The close helps the prospect make a decision that is good for him or her.

<u>The Trial Close</u>

1. A trial close tests the waters before you jump in to close.

2. Use it to find out if the prospect is ready to buy without actually asking if they are. If they aren't, then you can keep going with the sales process without putting it all at risk before it's time to do so.

3. If the trial close is positive, move at once, carefully, to a major close.

Sales

<u>Trial Close #1 Providing Choices</u>

Set up a pair or three choices for the prospect to pick one. If they pick one, it's a positive.

Example: You sell decorator pillows

You: "Do you think the blue, red, or the green will be best for your living room?

Prospect: "I don't know, maybe the blue would look good. Then again, maybe the red would too."

You: "So which will it be, the blue or the red?"

Result: Negative. "I can't decide, I'll have to sleep on it.

Neutral: "I wish I could afford both of them, but I can't."

Positive: "The blue; it'll fit right in with my arm chair." Close the sale

<u>Trial Close #2 Mistake On-Purpose</u>

Purposely make a mistake so the prospect can correct it.

Example: You: "So, Mrs. X, you said that the green one was the one you really like the most."

Prospect: "Oh no, I didn't say that. I don't like the green one at all.

You: "Well, which one do you like a lot?"

Prospect: "The blue, it will fit right in with my arm chair." Close the sale

<u>Trail Close #3 Feedback</u>

Ask a question that will get feedback from the prospect.

Example: Prospect: "Can I get these pillows in yellow?"

You: "So, you wish to have the yellow ones?"

Prospect: Negative: "No, I don't know yet."

Neutral: "I might, we'll see."

Positive: "Yes, that's right." Close the sale

<u>The Major Close</u>

1. Always ask a question, rather than make a statement

2. **Then, remain silent until the prospect answers. <u>The first one to speak loses!</u>**

3. **The prospect will either go along with you or give you a reason why not. Deal with the reason, the objection.**

Here are some common closing techniques:

<u>Assumptive Close</u>

You assume the prospect will buy. You then do something to start the buying process, like asking for a credit card number, or asking how s/he wants it delivered, or the address to which it is to be delivered, etc. This starts a flow that the prospect then has to do something to reverse.

<u>Start Writing Close</u>

You pull out the order form, or the contract, and at the right moment you simply start writing it up. This starts a flow that the prospect then has to do something to stop.

<u>String of Yesses Close</u>

You keep asking the prospect some simple, easy to answer questions, all of which you know will get a "yes" answer. Then, after the last question, you go for the close, expecting another yes.

<u>Run the Numbers Close</u>

You do the calculations and come up with a bottom line figure that you know will please the prospect. This can be combined with any of the other closes.

<u>Get the O.K. Close</u>

Rough out the deal, on a piece of scratch paper. Get the prospect to "O.K." it in theory. Then put it on an order form.

Sales

Ben Franklin Close (Balance Sheet close)

Take a plain sheet of paper and draw a line vertically down the middle. On the top of the left hand side write "yes". On the top of the right hand side write "No". Give your pen to the prospect. Ask prospect to list all of the reasons why s/he should make a decision to buy. Help with this. Then have the prospect list any "no's" on the other side, with no help from you. When finished, you say, "Well, it's pretty obvious isn't it?" Start writing it up.

Fear of Loss Close

You tell a story about a prospect, very much like the one you are with, who had a chance to buy and didn't. Point out all of the negative results of that prospect's decision not to buy.

This or That Close

To avoid asking a closing question that will get you a yes or no answer, you present two or three choices that the prospect is asked to select from among. Begin with, "Which do you prefer…?"

Apology Close

If you sense you have lost the sale, tell prospect you're really sorry you messed it up; that you know it would be of great benefit to the prospect. Ask what it was you did that messed it up.

1 to 10 Close

Ask the prospect, "On a scale of 1 to 10, how important is it to you to get rid of your frustration/anxiety/fear?

Think Some More Close

Prospect says, "I'll think it over." You say, "Just to help me be clear in my own thinking, what is it you will be thinking over; is it the integrity of my company, or my personal integrity, or something about my product/service, or the money? (memorize this). Keep on asking until you get down to the real issue.

3 + 1 Close

You remind the prospect that there are only three obvious questions: a. Do you like it? b. Do you want it? c. Can you afford it? If it looks like you get a "yes" to all three, then you say, "Well, there's only one more question. When do you want to start enjoying the benefits of it?"

Money-Money-Money Close

You ask the prospect three money questions: a. Can you see how this will save you money? b. Do you like to save money? c. If you were going to begin saving money, when would be the best time to start saving?

Inquiry Close

At just the right moment you ask the prospect, "Well, what shall we do next?"

Now or Never Close

You tell the prospect that it is definitely in his/her interest to buy right now, since XXX is going to happen, which will cause YYY to happen. XXX is a slight change, or a shortage of supply. YYY is a price change.

Feel-Felt-Found Close

Use this only once during a sales presentation. Use it only after you have found the real objection, the main thing getting in the way of the sale.

Example: Prospect: "I keep telling you, I don't have enough money for it right now."

You: "So, what I hear you saying is that you really feel that you can't afford this right now. I can appreciate that you *feel* that way. A lot of business people I speak to have felt that way. But what they have found was, when we took an in-depth look at how much money I can save them, it looked to them that it would actually pay for itself. Let me show you some numbers on this."

31 Possible Reasons Why There Was No Sale

1. Your company is not well known

2. Your company has a bad reputation

3. The prospect was not feeling well/in a bad mood

4. Your product/service is really not that good

5. Your company's positioning in the marketplace is off

6. The prospect said s/he didn't have enough money

7. The advertising hyped the quality of the product too much

8. The salesperson blew it. A good salesperson would pick this one

9. Did not have a script for the cold call to get the appointment (if applicable)

10. Did not practice doing the script (if applicable)

11. Did not actively listen enough

12. Talked too much

The One Person Business

13. Focused on self, not on prospect

14. Did not ask for the order

15. Did not anticipate objections

16. Did not defuse the objections

17. Tried to sell it, instead of guiding prospect to sell it to himself

18. Hurried the presentation

19. Went way over the time set for it

20. Forgot to ascertain type of prospect/customer s/he was dealing with

21. Let the prospect take control of the presentation

22. Tried to sell when getting the appointment

23. Tried to sell in step 2 of the 3 steps

24. Let fear run the presentation

25. Forgot to "mirror" the prospect

26. Screwed up the close

27. Talked features, not benefits

28. Was not willing to risk enough

29. Brought the wrong paperwork

30. Got too emotional

Put a √ by the ones you need to work on

Handling Objections

Often your prospect will voice one or more (usually more) objections. These are reasons why he or she won't or cannot buy now. They must be handled and overcome, otherwise there will be no sale.

<u>Do Not:</u>

1. Try to talk him/her out of it

2. Argue about it

3. Try to diffuse it if you only hear it once; it's probably not a real objection

<u>Do:</u>

1. Ask that it be repeated, so you know you understand what the objection is

2. Isolate the objection; make sure it's the only thing left in the way of the sale

3. Show prospect/customer that you understand it

4. Put the responses below on 3x5 cards and practice them a lot

5. Try to prevent the objection in advance

Neutralize it: Competitor does something—so do you

Off-set it: Competitor does it, you don't—we have an advantage that makes that less important

Displace it: Competitor does it—it's not what it appears to be; our way is better

There are some responses to common objections in Appendix R. Many of them take practice and courage, but they are time-tested to produce the result you want, which is to close the sale.

Asking Questions

If selling is about listening, then it is important to know how to ask questions. Here are some types of questions to use.

Open Ended Questions (the best kind; never a yes or no question)
These make the prospect give an answer in more than one or two words. They start with words such as:
Describe... Compare... How... Why... Explain... Tell me... What...
Example: What do you think about that? How will this help you meet your goals?

Closed Ended Questions Use them to make it easy for the prospect to warm up to you. Use them to obtain specific information. They start with words such as:
Will... Which... Is... Can... Who... Does... When... Are...
Example: Will this help you a lot? Do you want to order now?

Sales

<u>Anxiety Questions</u> Use them to see if the prospect is at all anxious about not getting the benefits of your product/service. Don't call it a problem; refer to him or her missing getting the benefits. Ask how much concern they have, not whether they have any or not. Anxiety questions focus on words such as:

Worries… issues… frustrations… irritations… hurdles… doubts… inconveniences…obstacles…difficulties

<u>Benefit Questions</u> Use them to make sure that the customer knows and understands the benefit(s) your product/service will bring.

Example: How does it feel to know that you'll never have to worry about the cost of rust-related maintenance again?

<u>Clarifying Questions</u> Use them to get the prospect to be less vague.

Example: Prospect: "It happens a lot?" You: "How often?" Prospect: "It takes too long." You: "How long is too long?"

<u>Rhetorical Questions:</u> Use them when you already know the answer but you want to get agreement on it.

They start with or include words such as:

Couldn't it… Doesn't it… Isn't it… Wouldn't you… Don't you agree…

Example: You'd expect to pay a lot more for this wouldn't you? Or, it makes good sense, doesn't it?

<u>Cost Questions</u> Use these to defuse objections to the price. Remember, there are 3 kinds of costs:

a. money costs b. frustration costs c. emotional costs

Example of each: a. What do those delays actually cost you? b. Why type of frustration does that cause you? c. How do you feel about that issue?

<u>Expectation Questions</u> Use them to get the prospect to expect good things from your product/service.

Example: I think you're really going to like these new widgets; that'll get rid of some of your frustrations won't it? Which ones will it get rid of?

Remember:

1. **In any sales presentation you might use many of these**

83

2. You may use them more than once

3. You probably won't use all of them in every presentation, but you could

4. They keep the prospect talking and you listening; that's good

Listening To Your Prospects/Customers (after you ask good questions)

There are two ways to listen: passively and actively. Active listening means that you interact with the speaker; you get some feedback from the speaker that you have heard him/her correctly.

This shows the speaker that you are not only listening, but also, that you are hearing him/her. It increases the comfort level of the speaker.

<u>Techniques of Active Listening</u>

<u>Repeating</u> If the prospect/customer says "I'd rather meet at 3 instead of at 5", you say "At 3 at your office."

<u>Accepting</u> When the prospect/customer says something, you say, "I see" or "I understand" or "Yeah, right." Not every time they say something, but periodically.

<u>Reflecting</u> If the prospect/customer says something in an excited manner, you say, "Yes, it's exciting." If the prospect/customer says that something is frustrating, you say, "Yes, it can be very frustrating."

<u>Paraphrasing</u> If the prospect/customer says, "It isn't going to be the same as it used to be", you say, "So, it's going to be different than it was, right?"

<u>Clarifying</u> If the prospect/customer says, "We may not be able to order for a while", you say, "Would that be days, weeks, or months?"

Sales

<u>Summarizing</u> If the prospect/customer has rattled off a long list of things or ideas, you say, "Let me be sure I understand everything you've said" and then you repeat back what you heard in summary form.

It is also good listening technique to "mirror" the speech pattern of the prospect/customer. For example:

1. If he/she speaks fast, you speak fast too

2. If he/she speaks loudly, you speak loudly too (he may be hard of hearing)

3. If he/she speaks softly, you speak softly too.

4. If he/she speaks very slowly, you speak slowly too.

5. If he/she speaks with his hands a lot, you do so too (but not too much)

6. If he/she says "I see how it could", you reply with "I <u>see</u> what you mean", using the <u>eye</u> word.

7. If he/she says, "It sounds good to me", you reply with "I <u>hear</u> you", using the <u>ear</u> word.

8. If he/she says "It feels good to me", you reply with "I get the <u>feeling</u> you like it", using the <u>feel</u> word. Mirror the word the prospect/customer uses.

9. Sales is not about talking

10. Listen to what your prospect/customer is not saying

11. **Listen to his/her objections and meet them at once**

12. **Listen to the body language**

13. **Listen to the tone, timbre, pace of your voice**

14. **Listen to whose side you're on**

15. **Listen to your script on tape**

16. **Listen to your sales results records; numbers tell the story**

Rating Your Customers

How does my business rate with my customer? That question is on the mind of most entrepreneurs. Suppose, however, that it's a two way street. There is just as great a need for the business owner to rate the customer. All customers are customers, but not all customers are equal. Some take very little of your time-energy-money, while others are very high maintenance customers/clients. They take a lot of your time and energy and don't buy much. Give them less of your time and energy.

Value for Value Relationships

Small business owners and corporate managers want their customers to feel that the company is giving them value; value-added product and service, as well as quality at a good price. Most of the time, however, very little if any attention is paid by the company to how much or how little value the customer is bringing to the relationship with the company.

Statements like the following are commonplace in reference to customers: "Oh, they're really a great customer", or "They order every week", or "They buy lots of stuff from me", or "They made a really big order".

Sales

The problem is that none of those statements reflect any determination as to how much value the customer has to your company. Those statements lead to an overly positive perception of the value of the customer. It's about how much they spend, sure, but it's also about how often they spend, and how much of your time they take, and if they take a lot of your energy, and so on.

While it is obviously good to have customers give feedback on how much value the company has to them, it is also good, and necessary, for the company to determine the quantity of value that each customer has for the company.

It's Not Just About Sales Volume

Sure it's good to have a customer that buys often, who buys in large amount. But business is not about sales; it's about profits. Many companies have lots of sales but no profits. Some of them treat all customers as if they have equal value to the company, when in fact they don't.

Even though a customer buys often, he may not buy very much. Even though he buys a big amount, he may not buy often. Even though he buys a lot, and quite often, he may buy items that have a smaller margin. Even though he buys a high margin item or items, he may not pay his bill for months. Even though he pays quickly, he may return a bunch of the product from every order. You get the picture.

By not knowing the true value of every customer, the business may be spending more time-money/energy with less valuable customers than with more valuable ones, and that costs money!

Track It and Rate It

In order to really determine the value of a customer, you need to create a system with which to rate your customers. Not all customers can be rated; it depends on the kind of business it is, and whether you can get the data. A rating has to be based upon more than your perceptions; it has to be based on quantified data. There are at least five factors that go into it:

1. Gross volume of purchases in a given time period

2. Average gross margin on the items purchased

3. Rate at which invoices get paid, slow or on time

4. Number of referrals given for new prospects

5. Amount of merchandize canceled or returned

First, give a weight to each factor. Give it a 3 if the factor is most important to you, 2 to the next most, 1 to the rest. Then, take each of those five factors and rate each customer on a scale of 1-3 or 1-5 for each factor.

Then multiply the score for each factor by the weight you gave to each factor, 1, 2, or 3.

Then add up the score for that customer. This will give you a composite score that lets you know how valuable to you that customer is in relation to other customers.

You can, if you wish, create a scale of ranges, wherein the highest range of scores gets an "A", the next highest a "B", the next highest range get s a "C", and the lowest a "D". This will make it easier to utilize the score.

Keep a File

In your computer, or in your files, keep a file on each customer that shows the composite rating score for that customer. This will enable you to make informed decisions about things like how much time to spend with the customer, how flexible to be in negotiations, how much money to spend on that customer for marketing purposes, to keep the customer or to get more sales.

Be sure to re-evaluate periodically to account for changes in the customer's behavior. It would be a disservice both to yourself and to the customer to not do so.

Sales

<u>Try It, You'll Like It</u>
Don't take my word for this. Try it out and see for yourself how valuable a tool a customer rating system can be. You may discover that your perceptions about your customers were misleading you, and this will give you a chance to correct those perceptions, replacing them with facts. How 'bout that?

Assessing Sales Results

Every company has a sales process, whether they have it documented or not, whether they use it consciously or not. Take a look at yours by answering the following: {Put a √ by the most appropriate answer, the one that occurs most often.} This is not for retail sales.

1. **Who does the selling in your company?**
   ❏ owner ❏ sales manager ❏ salesperson ❏ written materials

2. **How many steps are there in your sales process?**
   ❏ one step ❏ two steps ❏ three steps ❏ more

3. **What kind of sales are made the most?**
   ❏ one time sale ❏ repeat sales ❏ add-on sales ❏ upgrade sales

4. **Who picks the time of sale?**
   ❏ by chance ❏ by appointment ❏ customer picks ❏ company picks

5. **Where is the location where the sale takes place?**
   ❏ at customers ❏ at company office ❏ on the phone ❏ on the web

The One Person Business

6. **How tangible and low cost is the product or service you sell?**
   ☐ tangible and low cost ☐ tangible and high cost
   ☐ intangible and low cost ☐ intangible and high cost

7. **How readily accessible is your product or service?**
   ☐ buyer gets it on the spot ☐ buyer picks it up later
   ☐ buyer gets it delivered later

8. **How is paid for?**
   ☐ Buyer gets extended credit terms, no interest charged
   ☐ credit with interest charged ☐ onto a credit card
   ☐ buyer pays all cash

For each question, the choice farthest to the left is the easiest selling situation, and the one farthest to the right is the most difficult in which to make the sale.

Give yourself 3 points for a left hand choice, 2 points for a middle choice, and 1 point for a far right-hand choice. Add up your total.

Rating: 24 to 20=easy selling situation

19 to 12=a mixed bag; consider some changes

11 to 8 =a difficult selling situation; make some changes

7 to 0 =next to impossible

Now that you have plenty to think about, study, and practice for your marketing and sales, let's turn to the third component, operations.

Operations

Now we come to the component that's about what the business does, what it delivers to the customer, be it a product or a service. The key to this component of your one-person small business is systems. Unless you have systems in place, in writing, you will need to reinvent the wheel over and over again. You will also have a much harder time selling the business if and when that time comes, since it is your systems that the buyer of your business will buy.

A system can be very complex or it can be a simple checklist. Many good systems are just that, a checklist that you and/or someone else can follow if you are sick, on vacation, or in an emergency.

Any good system will tell the following: When will it be performed? What is the result to be obtained? How is it to be performed; what are the steps?

Systematizing Your Small Business

1. **Any successful business has systems**

2. **Every successful business has systems**

The One Person Business

<u>Why?</u>

1. Systems allow you to eventually replace yourself with employees (if you choose to)

2. Systems bring order to the chaos

3. Systems help you prevent overwhelm

<u>How?</u>

1. Use a checklist format-each step clearly defined

2. Keep them in proper sequence

<u>What to Systematize</u>

Banking-money in/money out-petty cash – bookkeeping – marketing - sales process-phone answering – budgeting – billing – projections – receiving – filing – shipping - taking orders – collections - ordering supplies and materials – inventory - work flow, etc. etc. etc.

You will undoubtedly have some not on that list, and some that are on the list will not apply to your business. Whereas cash is the lifeblood of your business, systems are the bone structure of the business.

<u>Guides</u>

1. Stick to every system until you change it in writing

2. Change them as needed to improve them

3. Create new ones as you grow the business

Work Flow

If your operations are complex then it is a good idea to create a workflow chart. Start at the first step and diagram what happens in each step, in detail. Each step should describe the task and the steps to perform it. The last step should tell where it goes to the next step in the workflow. Doing a good job on this will help you to not have to remember it each time you do it. It will also bring clarity to your mind about it.

Many one-person business owners get so busy doing the work that they forget or fail to do the systematizing of the business. They are working *in* the business, but not *on* the business. A real entrepreneur does both, and eventually hires people (if you choose to) to work in the business, or outsources the task, thus freeing him or herself to work *on* the business. Working *on* the business is doing the strategy, doing the planning, making the big decisions, charting the growth, tracking the numbers, analyzing the financial reports, and so on.

If you do not work on the business, not just in it, you will not successfully grow the business, and you most likely will cause it to fail. The book *The E Myth* by Michael Gerber is an excellent explanation of this concept.

Administration

This is the office stuff. It too needs to be systematized, and the workflow charted. Good forms, good files, good records, good reporting, good ordering systems are all part of good administration.

Having an orderly process, a clear process, a well functioning system will help you keep your mind uncluttered. It will make it unnecessary for you to try to remember everything in your head. That will prevent things from falling through the cracks.

Well functioning administration is important to the other four components. A great marketing system, sales system, operations system and financial system are the main goal of administration. It supports the other four components.

Eventually, if you wish to grow your business beyond a one-person business, you will need to outsource functions in the business. Things like bookkeeping, sales, admin assistant, and so on.

The key to outsourcing is this; stop doing what you do not like to do or what you are not good at. Then you can focus on what you do like to do. Do this as soon as you can afford it, *if* you wish to grow beyond a one-person business. It will probably be possible for you to outsource certain functions

The One Person Business

and still remain a one-person business, if that's your choice. You will get to the point, I hope, where you have to decide whether or not to remain a one-person business. There are good arguments in favor of each scenario.

Finance

Now we come to the last of the five components. This is, perhaps, the second most important of the five. Business is about money. Money is about numbers. Finance is about money numbers. There are three financial projections that need to be done. They are budget projections, sales projections, and cash flow projections. Without these you will not have a clue about the money part of your business.

The budget projections and the cash flow projections are pretty easy to do. The sales projections are not, since they are more of a guess. The goal is to make the guess an educated guess, based on your market research and the assumptions you make. We will begin with the budget projections.

3 Projections to Make

<u>Budget Projections</u>

For Startups you need to prepare a *Pro forma* budget as part of your start-up planning. It gives you a forecast of the future. It lets you know how much money you'll need to operate your new business until it starts to make a profit.

The One Person Business

For ongoing businesses, "guestimating" the future will help you make long-term decisions. It gives you a basis for plans.

You should make three of everything; one based on a "best case" scenario and one based on a "worst case" scenario, and the third a merging of the first two.

You should be realistic and be conservative. It's better to have it turn out better than you thought it would.

For Start-Ups

1. Do the best you can. It won't be perfect. Good enough is enough.

2. Look at each line item by itself.

3. Be realistic. Do not overestimate an expense, but also, do not grossly underestimate it. Better to overestimate.

4. Do the annual first, and then do the monthlies.

5. Remember, the purpose of this, combined with your sales projection and cash flow projection, is to arrive at how much money you'll need to operate the business until it starts to make a profit.

6. Determine in your mind what Net Profit percent you wish to earn. Be reasonable. 25% is much too high. Between 5% and 10% is realistic.

7. If it doesn't "work" the first time, recalculate, re-estimate, and do it again. Lower your Net Profit %, or raise your Gross Profit %, or rethink your expenses, line by line, and lower some of them, or do all of these.

Finance

<u>For Ongoing Business</u>

1. Do the best you can. It won't be perfect. Good enough is enough.

2. Look at each line item by itself.

3. Be realistic. Do not overestimate an expense, but also, do not grossly underestimate it. Better to overestimate.

4. Use input from everyone; customers, accountant, banker, trade journal, trade association, suppliers.

5. Round off the percentages.

6. Determine in your mind what Net Profit percent you wish to earn. Be reasonable. 25% is much too high. Between 5% and 10% is realistic.

7. If it doesn't "work" the first time, recalculate, re-estimate, and do it again. Lower your Net Profit %, or raise your Gross Profit %, or rethink your expenses, line by line, and lower some of them, or do all of these.

8. It is o.k. to trade-off, to lower one item and then raise another one or vice-versa.

9. Do your Annual Budget projection first, and then do the monthlies.

10. Combine past year's performance with your "guestimate" of future periods and merge the two in your mind.

The One Person Business

11. If you've been in business for at least two years, do not include figures from the current year.

12. As the year ahead unfolds, readjust/redo your budget based on actual numbers.

Sales Projections

This is not easy, because you are just starting and you have no sales records. However, there is a way to create a reasonable guesstimate.

Here is what you do:

1. Compute what your Cost of Goods Sold will be for each unit you will sell (or, if a service business, for each contract or service delivery). This is not easy, because you need to estimate how much revenue your <u>average</u> sale will bring in, but try).

2. Multiply the dollar figure for COGS per unit (or average sale) times the number of units (or dollars of sales) you need to break even. This gives you the dollar amount of variable costs for all of the sales you'll make in the next 12 months.

3. Now, compute what your total Overhead Expenses will be for the year.

4. Add the COGS and Overhead Expenses together. The total is your Break-Even sales dollar figure. Call that "B".

5. Multiply that figure, "B" by 50%. Call that answer "A".

6. Now, take "B" and multiply it by 125%. Call the answer "C".

Finance

7. **Next, do this:**

    Multiply "A" times 3. Call the answer "X".
    Multiply "B times 6 Call the answer "Y".
    Multiply "C" times 3. Call the answer "Z".
    Add "X" and "Y" and "Z" together, This is your projected annual start-up sales projection figure.

Here are some suggestions for you to think about when you're making sales projections if you are an ongoing business. The assumptions you make will directly affect your projections. Will it stay the same, go up or down, and if so, by how much. Be conservative.

1. **Sales effort** - Will more time be put into selling? Will your territory expand or contract?

2. **Competition** - Will there be more next year or maybe less? How will this affect your pricing? Your sales?

3. **Adding products/services** - Will there be any new ones added?

4. **Sales strategy** - Are you going to change your sales practices, sales mediums, etc.

5. **Advertising changes** - Going to do more? Less? Different kinds? New market targets?

6. **Price changes** - Raising or lowering them? Will this increase sales or lower them?

7. **Supplier changes** - Will their prices go up? Will you buy in bulk to get lower prices?

8. Abnormal sales - Did you have any super large one-time sales? Do you expect to this year?

9. Demographic changes - Will the mix of age, sex, income, education, etc. change in your market and affect sales?

10. Tax changes - Any anticipated? How will they affect your business?

11. Legal changes - Any new laws, regulations or ordinances coming into effect?

12. Economy factors - How will they affect your sales?

13. Interest rate changes - Will they affect your sales?

14. Physical changes - Moving to a new location; adding new equipment; making improvements to site; how will these affect your sales?

15. Any others adjustments you can think of.

Cash Flow Projections

This is not hard to do. You will use your budget projections and sales projections to do it. You can find templates to use for all three projections on the website of most SBDC offices. Here are the steps for cash flow projections:

1. Complete your sales projections.

2. Complete your budget projections.

Finance

3. Calculate your starting cash balance. This will be how much actual cash you have on hand, <u>after</u> you have paid for your startup costs.

4. Put the starting cash number at the top of the first month for which you are doing this projection.

5. Add to this number the total sales revenues and any other income that will come in during the first month.

6. Subtract, from this starting cash balance cash + income, the total of the budget expenses that will take money out of the business.

7. This is best done with a list of the expenses, as they will change from month to month, since all bills do not get paid on a monthly basis.

8. You will now have your ending cash balance for the first month of the projection. This number becomes the starting cash balance for the next month.

9. Continue steps 5, 6, and 7 for each month until you have done it for all 12 months.

10. If any month has a negative ending cash balance it means that you will not be able to pay your bills for that month. You will need to improve your cash flow.

Note: It is helpful to do a 'rolling cash flow' projection. This is where you recalculate each month, using the current month as the first month on the chart and then project out twelve months forward from that month.

The Money Numbers

Calculating Break Even

Perhaps the most critical financial number you need to know is your breakeven number. This lets you know if you are making any profit or not.

The best way to calculate this is in terms of revenue, unless you can clearly know how many units will be sold. Breakeven point is where the total revenues = the total expenses. No profit, no loss.

Break Even Formula

Perhaps the most critical financial number you need to know is your "Breakeven" point or Breakeven Sales point. The Breakeven Sales point is that point in your sales cycle when your sales revenues exactly equal your total costs. Your total costs are the sum of your variable costs and your fixed costs. Once the Breakeven Point is reached, each additional unit sold results in profit before taxes.

The Breakeven Sales (BE Sales) may be calculated in terms of either sales in dollars (revenues) or sales in units. If you calculate one of these you can easily calculate the other. BE Sales for a product-based business is different from a service-based business, mainly due to the presence of variable costs with a product-based business. The steps to calculate BE Sales are shown below.

A. Product Based Business

1. **Identify your Sales Price per Unit. For a multi-product business calculate an average Sales Price per Unit. For a one product business, just take the sales price of it. For example, assume a Sale Price (SP) of $80.**

Finance

2. Calculate your Variable Cost per Unit: Cost of Goods Sold plus Variable Selling Costs. Cost of Goods sold (COGS) is the sum of direct materials, direct labor, & manufacturing overhead.

   Variable Selling Costs are generally sales commissions. (but not for a one person business since you are the salesperson) For a multi-product business calculate an average Variable Cost (VC) per unit. For our example assume COGS is $55 so VC= $55.

3. Next calculate your "Contribution Margin" per unit. Contribution Margin (CM) is the sale price per unit (or average sale price per unit if multi-unit) minus variable cost per unit. From the numbers above CM = SP - VC or CM = $25 ($80 - $55)

4. Next calculate your "Contribution Margin Ratio" (CM%) by dividing your CM by Sale Price, so CM% = 31% ($25 / $80)

5. Calculate your total Fixed Costs, e.g., rent, utilities, insurance, taxes, etc. Assume Fixed Costs (FC) = $150,000 for this example.

6. For Breakeven Sales in units divide Fixed Costs by the Contribution Margin, so the BE Sales in Units = FC / CM = 6,000 units ($150,000 / $25). You would need, in our example, to sell 6,000 units to break even.

B. For Breakeven Sales in Dollars for your product based business divide Fixed Costs by the Contribution Margin Ratio, so BE Sales in dollars = FC / CM% = $600,000 ($150,000 / .25).

If you first calculate BE Sales in units a simpler way to find BE Sales in dollars is to multiply the BE Sales in units by the sale price, so 6000 by $80 = $480,000. The opposite is also true; if you have BE Sales in dollars you can find BE Sales in units by dividing BE Sales in dollars by the sale price, so $480,000 / $80 = 6,000 units.

C. Service Based Business

1. To calculate the Breakeven Sales in dollars for a service-based business you can revise the calculations above for a product based business by removing the variable costs.

2. Thus the BE Sales in dollars = Total Fixed Costs.

3. To calculate the BE Sales in Units for a service based business, divide the BE Sales in Dollars by the Unit Sale Price. The unit sale price would be the average dollar amount of your average contract (job). This lets you know how many contracts you need to have to break even.

Financial Analysis
The 3 Documents You Must Have
1. Balance Sheet

2. Profit & Loss Statement

3. Cash Flow Chart

What Each Does

1. Balance Sheet - It shows what the company owns (assets) and what it owes (liabilities) and the owners equity in the business (net worth) *on a given date*. It contains everything in your

company that can be given a dollar value, things both tangible and intangible. It is for a given date.

2. Profit & Loss Statement - It gives you the "bottom line" after you subtract all of the expenses and costs from the total of all of the income. It covers a period of time, usually a month, a quarter, or a year.

3. Cash Flow - This tracks the flow of money into and out of the business. It lets you know how well you will be able to meet your cash needs to pay your bills, and whether you need a short term loan or cash infusion or not.

<u>Why You Need Them</u>

1. You cannot manage your business if you don't know how you're doing, if your financial status is vague or unknown.

2. You can't make good decisions if you don't know what's happening.

3. Your banker will require them

4. It brings clarity, which brings confidence

<u>Tips</u>

1. Do your Profit & Loss Statement weekly if you are a new business; do it monthly for sure.

2. Pay attention to the ratios that the Balance Sheet and P&L Statement will provide you.

3. You should maintain cash balances equal to two weeks of sales as a "cushion".

Assets are what your company owns. Liabilities are what it owes. Owner's equity (net worth) is what is left after the liabilities are subtracted from the assets. Thus, A=L+E also A-L=E

If you are just starting to use the Balance Sheet and don't have all the numbers do the best you can to reconstruct them. Use the current market values of your assets; use the total amount of profits retained in the business. Start keeping accurate records now.

Money Advice

<u>Improving Your Cash Flow</u>

Let's say you're making lots of sales; your profit margins are excellent; but you're always short of cash to pay the bills. This is a common problem of many small business owners. Here are some tips:

1. Get the billings out the door more quickly

2. Be sure to put due dates on all bills sent out

3. Rework your cash flow projections

4. Send more reminders to those late to pay

5. Give a discount for payment in cash

6. Get a line of credit to borrow against for short term needs

Finance

7. Shorten the net term for payment

8. Let the customer make electronic payment into your account

9. Send the bill to the person who actually pays it in the company it's sent to

10. Pay your suppliers on a schedule, rather than all at once

11. Figure out how to sell off old inventory or reduce inventory needs

12. Buy supplies and inventory in smaller amounts

Collecting the Money Customers Owe You

For one reason or another, many businesses have money that is owed to them. No surprise there. The trick is to collect it. The best way to make sure you can collect it is to take precautions <u>before</u> it is owed to you.

For example:

1. Check out the credit of those who are going to owe you, if it's a big amount. You are really loaning them money if they don't pay cash. Do so with caution.

2. Ask for a financial statement. If they are buying for the first time, make sure they have the money before you ship it to them.

3. Be sure the terms of the sale are in writing, clear, and fair to both you and your customer.

The One Person Business

If you've done all that, and you loaned the money by giving them credit terms, and they are late in paying you, then do these things:

1. **Bill them in a timely manner. Do not let days and days go by. Send the bill promptly.**

2. **Enforce the carrying charge/interest you put in the contract when you made the sale.**

3. **Call them up and give them an incentive to pay you right away, like a discount of a future purchase.**

4. **Send them a letter that includes:**

    - **reference to the contract/agreement**

    - **total balance due**

    - **due date for payment**

    - **address for payment**

    - **an invitation to discuss it**

    - **desire to be fair**

    - **note of appreciation for their business**

    - **Insist that they pay now or you will not be able to ship again until they do.**

Finance

<u>Tips</u>

1. Track the aging of your accounts receivables on a regular schedule-daily, weekly, monthly as need be.

2. Don't wait more than 45 days to go into action to collect it. The older it gets the harder it is to collect.

3. Turn it over to a collection agency only as a last resort. It will lose you the customer forever, and cost you the collection fee they charge.

4. If you offer a discount if they pay now put it in plain English. If it isn't paid promptly, send a photocopy a week later that indicates when the discount period will end.

5. Make calls to collect early in the week.

6. Always talk to the person who signs the checks.

7. Always address the customer by name.

8. Give them a chance to explain; the reason for being late may be acceptable.

9. Try to get a firm commitment for a partial payment.

10. If they agree to pay, all or part, send them a letter confirming and formalizing their agreement to pay.

Guide to Borrowing Money

1. Know exactly how much you need to borrow.

2. Know specifically what you are going to use it for. Make a list.

3. Know specifically how you are going to repay it.

4. Have a plan B that tells how you will repay it if things do not work out.

Establishing credit credibility:

1. Get your credit report as clean as possible

2. Pay all your suppliers in a timely manner

3. Keep your credit card debt as low as possible

4. Do not have too many credit cards

Sources of Money

1. Mercy Money - Your family member or friend loans you the money at a low interest rate.

2. Credit Card Funds - You do a cash advance on your credit card(s). This is high interest money. You can play "credit card roulette" with low APR intro rates, but sooner or later you are stuck paying the high interest rate.

Finance

3. Short-Term Credit - The bank provides a short-term loan for a specific reason, for less than a year. An example would be a loan to help you buy inventory for the next selling season.

4. Trade credit - This is not a loan. You get your suppliers to give you an open account to carry your fast-moving inventory.

5. Long-Term Credit - A loan for more than a year to use for expansion or remodeling. To be repaid out of profits. Secured by a mortgage or promissory note with terms.

6. Equity Funds - You assign part of your profits to an investor. You sell a part of your business to the investor. This is not a loan.

Alternatives to Borrowing

1. Increase your sales by improving marketing and sales efforts.

2. Be more diligent in collecting your accounts receivables.

3. Control your expenses better.

4. Do better cash forecasting.

5. Get your suppliers to extend your payment terms.

6. Draw less money from the business each month

Conclusion

I have tried to write a book that will not just be read, but will be used. That is why the sections in each component are mostly lists of tips and lists. Some of them can be put into use immediately, and some you will use as your business grows.

I have done very little with Administration. The key is to have good systems, and whatever works for you will be fine. No systems = chaos.

I have purposely omitted a section on hiring. I did this on the assumption that a one-person business usually remains a one-person business, sometimes by choice, sometimes by necessity.

I will appreciate any feedback you might be moved to give, positive or negative. Email your thoughts to lsimon@shentel.net.

If you would like to have a digital copy of this book simply send a request by email to lsimon@shentel.net I will send it to you right away. You can then download specific pages for your use.

I have owned two successful small businesses, for a total of 32 years. In that time I have learned a great many things about people and about business. That is one of the biggest perks of owning a one person business.

I want to wish you much success in your business. It takes the 3D's and the 3R's and a bit of luck. I hope you have a whole lot of all of those.

Appendix A

Pros of Buying an Existing Business

    It may be less risky than a startup

    Probably profitable more quickly than a startup

    Established name, location, staff, customers, licenses, etc.

    You may find a seller who is desperate to sell and get a really good deal on it.

    You do not have to go through all of the hassles of starting it up.

    It has proven itself to be a money-maker.

    It will have an established customer/client base.

    You won't have to search for a location for it.

    It may have been poorly managed or have potential that has not been realized yet.

    You may get the benefit of the seller's experience in the business and the community if he or she stays around to train you.

<u>Disadvantages</u>

    Most businesses that are being sold are not doing very well. Why doesn't a relative want it?

    The seller may have been cooking the books and is deceiving you.

The One Person Business

When it changes hands some or many customers may leave.

If you use a business broker some or all of his commission will be added into the purchase price.

Changing the location can be expensive.

There may be some technical knowledge or skill that the owner has that you don't know about and don't have.

It might be less likely to be something for which you have passion.

You will probably think you can run it better than they did, and that may not be so.

It may be in the wrong location

The owner may have a bad reputation

The inventory may be of a different quality than you want

You may not like the fixtures and equipment and furniture

It is a horse trading negotiation and you may get shafted.

You buy the assets <u>and</u> the liabilities of the business

You may be paying for their mistakes and inefficiencies

The seller's estimate of 'goodwill' may be very inflated

They may value inventory at retail instead of at cost

The reason given as to why they are selling may not be the real reason

<u>Should you use a Business Broker?</u>

<u>Yes</u>

They have experience with lots of kinds of businesses.

They can help you determine the fair market value of the business.

They function as a go-between in the negotiations with the seller.

They know about a lot of businesses that are for sale.

<u>No</u>

Only half of all small businesses that are sold are sold through a business broker. Why?

How do you know if you can trust the broker to tell you the truth all the time?

Appendix A

They don't have the really good businesses; they get the ones that are hard to sell.

They may only show you the listings from their own office.

Here are 3 methods to determine Valuation of the Business

1. **Adjusted Balance Sheet Method**

The value of the owner's equity: net worth=assets-liabilities

Adjust the actual market value of the assets

Adjust for goodwill, sweat equity, name equity, on-going contracts

2. **Market Valuation Method**

What a comparable business sold for in the last 6 months

Sold in the local market

Valued at "X" times the after-tax earnings for latest year (having the right "X" is critical)

What a willing buyer and willing seller agree on

3. **Earnings Based Method**

Uses audited financial statements, which will determine if the "books are cooked".

Adjust for unusual practices, items, changes

Watch out for these: unusual expense items - undesirable assets – under-insured - increase in rent upon sale - obsolete inventory - etc.

Calculate the capitalization rate three times based on small, moderate or high risk. Apply a capitalization rate of 15% small risk; 25% moderate risk; 50% high risk; the cap rate is multiplied times the re-characterized earnings for the latest year. (If you don't understand this go see an accountant)

Don't ignore the risk from these: competition, owner's expertise/charisma, changes/trends in the industry, your learning curve, licenses and insurance needed.

The One Person Business

Ratios
  Using audited statements, calculate the following ratios:
  Liquidity current assets/current liabilities
  Debt to Equity (safety) total liabilities/equity
  Profitability gross profit/sales
  Operating Performance 1 inventory turnover=COGS/inventory
  Also Day's A/R = 365/A/R Turnover
  Here are the key things to consider:
  Location
  Industry
  Fit with your experience
  Match to interests
  Purchase price
  Fit with buyer's goals
  Income potential
  Future potential
  Supports your lifestyle
  Independent vs. Franchise business

It's a good idea to be represented by a business attorney or a business broker if you choose to buy an existing business. Here is a list of 65 questions to ask the seller. You will not need an answer to each and every one of them, as some of them will not apply.

65 Questions to Ask Before Buying Any Business

General Questions

1. **What turns you on about it and excites you?**

2. **How much time does it demand to run it?**

Appendix A

3. Can you own it without actually working in it?

4. Will it bring you the income you need; not want, need?

5. If it were not for sale, is this a business you would want to start up?

General Factors

6. How was the asking price arrived at?

7. What are the key ratios?

8. Why is it being sold?

9. Is it a documented business or just a job for the owner?

10. What is the asking price and what are the terms of sale?

11. Is it in a location that truly serves the needs of the type of business that it is?

12. Is there a good supply of labor available to meet the needs of the business if and when it may be needed?

13. Is the parking adequate to meet the needs?

14. When was the business started?

15. How many different owners has it had at this location?

16. How long has the present owner operated it?

17. Are there any current code or regulations violations?

18. Is the industry it is in a stable industry or a fad industry?

19. How seasonal or cyclical is the business?

20. Who are the suppliers/vendors?

21. How reliable are the suppliers/vendors?

22. Is there dependence on just one supplier/vendor?

23. How fierce is the competition?

24. Is the competition increasing or not?

25. What advantages does this business have over its competitors?

26. Are any of the competitors businesses for sale now?

Marketing Factors

27. Is there a clear idea of who the customer is?

28. How many customers are there in the market segment/area?

29. Is the current positioning strategy of the business adequate?

30. Is there a real method for setting prices?

31. Is the customer base rising or declining?

Appendix A

32. Will the customers stay after the new owner takes over?

33. Will the owner want the customer list after he/she no longer owns the business?

34. Is there an adequate marketing plan in place, with calendar and budget?

<u>Sales Factors</u>

35. How are the sales people trained if there are any?

36. How are the salespeople compensated?

37. How are the salespeople managed?

38. What are the year-to-year changes in sales?

39. If sales are increasing, why?

40. If sales are going down, why?

<u>Financial Factors</u>
   <u>Expenses</u>

41. Which are increasing as a percent of gross income?

42. Which are decreasing as a percent of gross income?

43. What are the ratios that apply to sales?

44. What is the owner's salary or draw?

45. Are the records of expenses accurate?

Profit

46. What are the gross profit ratios?

47. Are they in line with industry averages?

48. What are the net profit ratios?

49. Are they in line with industry averages?

50. Has the owner's salary been paid as a draw?

51. What is the break-even point for the business?

52. Is the net profit figure you are told a number **before** or after taxes?

Balance Sheet

53. What is the aging of the accounts receivable?

54. Are the accounts receivables owned by a few or by many of the customers?

55. Is there a good system for collecting them?

56. What is the present market value of each fixed asset?

Appendix A

57. Have the fixed assets been depreciated?

58. Are the accounts payable current?

59. How old are the debts?

60. Is the current ratio healthy?

61. Is the quick ratio healthy?

62. Is the ratio of assets to net worth healthy?

63. What is the amount of net worth?

64. Has the net worth been going up or down for the past 3 years?

65. Is the valuation placed on the goodwill realistic?

Tips {remember, some of the above questions will not apply if you will be a one- person business}.

Try to get the answers to the applicable questions in writing from the owner.

a. Rate each answer on a scale of 1 to 3. 3 is good; 2 is so-so; 1 is unsatisfactory.

b. Go through the list and pick out the questions that are "deal breakers" for you and put a check mark by each of them.

c. Compute a total score, but do not buy if one or more of the deal breakers is unsatisfactory.

1. Do not hurry the process of buying; it is better to lose out to another buyer than to make a bad buy.

2. Have a good accountant look at the financial answers. If, however, you decide that you want to buy a franchise, there are many things to consider. See Appendix B.

3. If you buy an existing business, don't keep the old name if the goodwill was overestimated. Don't create a new name if the goodwill was accurate or underestimated. Make your company name have marketing value. Do some market research to see if your potential customers like your new name before you change it. If most of them like it, use it, even if you don't like it very much.

Appendix B

Common Franchise Formats

1. Franchisor is the Producer/creator. You get to use the Franchisor's business name; you are a wholesaler.

2. Franchisor is a wholesaler. You are the retailer for their products.

3. Franchisor is Producer/Creator- Sells you an affiliate franchise, a business format franchise with a complete system. This is the most common.

<u>Pro's</u>
Turnkey operation
Can compete quickly
Known name and product/service
Access to experts
Increased purchasing power
National advertising
Avoids problems of starting from scratch

Business and operating plans and systems

<u>Con's</u>

You have to apply and qualify

You have to negotiate

You have to pay royalties, fees, and have audits

You have to buy product from the franchisor exclusively

You may be stuck owing on expensive equipment if you go out of business.

<u>Tips</u>

Retain a business attorney from day one; if you can't afford one you probably can't afford the franchise either

Beware of scams and near scams

You must use due diligence to check it out

Buyer beware!

Here is a list of questions to ask any franchisor; remember, not all of them will apply to every situation.

118 Questions To Ask When Buying A Franchise

<u>To Ask the Franchisor</u>

(Note: The franchisor's Disclosure Statement should provide the data for many of these answers)

1. **What is the identity of the franchisor?**

2. **Who are the officers of the franchisor?**

3. **Are there any lawsuits, past or present, against the franchisor?**

Appendix B

4. Are there any prior bankruptcies of the franchisor or officers?

5. How are any continuing payments (royalties) to be paid?

6. How good is the quality of goods/services to be purchased from the franchisor?

7. Is there any financial or other assistance from franchisor with franchise purchasing?

8. Are there any restrictions on the goods/services the franchisee (you) is permitted to sell?

9. Are there any restrictions on the customers with whom the franchisee may deal?

10. Is the territorial protection adequate to protect the franchisee?

11. Are the conditions under which the franchisor may refuse renewal of the franchise acceptable?

12. Are the conditions under which the franchisor may repurchase the outlet acceptable?

13. Are the restrictions on the franchisee's selling or transferring the outlet acceptable?

14. Are the terms of how either party may terminate the agreement acceptable?

15. Is the training program satisfactory?

16. Is the assistance of the franchisor in site selection satisfactory?

17. Is the statistical data on the number of existing franchises, projected franchises, and terminated franchises (repurchased or not renewed) satisfactory?

18. Is the franchisor's financial condition satisfactory?

19. Is the degree of personal participation required in the operation of the franchise by the franchisee satisfactory?

20. Is the projection of potential franchisee profits acceptable?

21. Is the number of franchises actually achieving those profits satisfactory?

22. Will you get a list of the names and addresses of existing franchisees with permission to contact them?

To Ask Existing Franchisees

23. When and why did you buy your franchise?

24. Why did you select this franchise over others that were available?

25. How effective was the training program?

26. Did the franchisor fulfill his obligations in setting up the franchise?

Appendix B

27. When you buy things from the franchisor, are deliveries on time and prices competitive?

28. How effective is your area supervisor?

29. How often does the supervisor visit you?

30. Have you and the supervisor had disagreements?

31. How effective is the advertising program?

32. Does your strongest competitor have advantages over you?

33. Do the sale and profit figures compare favorably to what you expected to earn?

34. Are your sales growing?

35. Are your profits growing?

36. Has the franchisor honored the franchise agreement? If not, how not?

37. Are the problems you have with the franchisor being resolved to your satisfaction?

38. How many other franchisees do you know?

39. Are those you know happy with the marketing program?

The One Person Business

40. Are they satisfied with the franchise?

41. Would they do it again today?

To Ask Failed Franchisees

42. Why did your franchise fail?

43. Was what the franchisor did to try to save it satisfactory?

44. Did the franchisor offer to repurchase the franchise on acceptable terms?

45. If the location was the problem, would you consider the same franchise in a different location?

<u>To Ask the Suppliers of the Franchise</u>

46. Are the franchisees required to buy from you?

47. Have orders for goods increased per franchise?

48. Do the franchisees pay their bills promptly?

49. Do you know any of the new product lines being considered?

50. How do prices compare to prices for non-franchised accounts?

<u>To Ask the Franchisor</u>

51. When will the franchise be available?

Appendix B

52. What locations are available?

53. If a franchise has ever been assigned to any of those areas, what happened to it?

54. What are the future plans for the franchise?

55. Can I have a sample franchise contract to review?

<u>To Ask of the Contract/Agreement Itself</u>

56. What will the franchise cost?

57. What are the initial franchise fees?

58. What are the ongoing royalties?

59. How often must I pay the royalties?

60. Are there any other hidden start-up costs?

61. What are the specifications of the physical plant?

62. What will the franchisor provide for the physical plant?

63. What will I have to provide for the physical plant?

64. What is the completion date?

65. What is the proposed territory?

66. What are my protections for the territory?

67. Who can compete with me?

68. Who finds the site?

69. Is the territory exclusive?

70. Who approves the site?

71. If I am required to work in the franchise, in what way?

72. What are the salary limitations?

73. Who controls the hours?

74. Who controls the product selection?

75. Are the sources of supply limited or controlled?

76. Are prices controlled?

77. Is layout controlled?

78. Are budgets or expenditures controlled?

79. What other policies or regulations will govern me?

80. Is there an operations manual I have to follow?

81. Can I advertise on my own?

Appendix B

82. What training will I receive?

83. What is the cost to me of the training?

84. Where is the location of the training?

85. How long does the training last?

86. Will I have any start-up assistance?

87. Who pays for a grand-opening launch?

88. What continuing supervision will I have?

89. Are any legal or accounting services provided?

90. Can I expect any other kind of support?

91. What are the local and/or national advertising plans?

92. Must I participate in all promotional programs?

93. Is there a separate advertising charge or fee?

94. Will the franchisor assist me in developing my own ads?

95. Can I sell my franchise?

96. Can I transfer my franchise?

97. Can I mortgage my franchise?

The One Person Business

98. Can I transfer my franchise upon my death?

99. What are the restrictions, if any, upon such transfer?

100. Does the franchisor have a repurchase option?

101. How long is the franchise period?

102. Is the franchise renewable?

103. What are the terms of renewal?

104. Do I pay a new franchise fee upon renewal?

105. Can I cancel the franchise?

106. What constitutes a default or breach?

107. Can I "cure" a default?

108. Do I have a "right of first refusal" on adjoining territories?

109. What financing will the franchisor provide?

110. What are the terms of that financing?

111. What security must I pledge for the financing?

112. Who is liable on the debt?

113. What remedies does the franchisor have if I default?

Appendix B

<u>To Ask Yourself</u>

114. **Are you willing to adhere to the company rules and policies?**

115. **Is this an industry that you actually have an interest in?**

116. **Have you established specific criteria for a franchise for you?**

117. **Have you reviewed all those that meet those criteria?**

118. **Has the franchisor thoroughly evaluated you to determine whether or not you are a suitable candidate for his franchise?**

Suggestion: "score" the answer to each question as follows:
A=acceptable B=questionable C=unsatisfactory

Given your personal specific needs and situation, go through the list and pick out the items that, for you, are "deal breakers". On those items, you would not buy, even if the scores are high on other factors.

<u>12 Biggest Mistakes Made by Prospective Franchise Owners</u>

These are the mistakes that cause prospective franchise owners the biggest headaches and problems. Each of them is avoidable with proper research and investigation to gather facts about franchisors.

#1 - **Not having an accurate personal pro-forma financial statement.**
You need to know how much money and how much cash you have to work with. No guesses. You need real numbers. Some franchises will be affordable to you and some won't. Don't waste your time with those that aren't. Know how much money you've got and what it will take to buy the franchise.

The One Person Business

#2 - Failure to create a cash reserve fund for working capital. It takes more than you think it will to run any business. Most new owners grossly underestimate, so it's a good idea to buy one that costs less than you can really afford; then you'll have some money left over as a back-up fund.

#3 - Not carefully reading and understanding the franchise agreement. You need to do three things to avoid this mistake: a) make or get a list of written questions to present to the franchisor (b) get answers in writing c) take the written answers to a good franchise attorney <u>before you sign anything</u>.

#4 - Not getting all representations made by the franchisor in writing. If it isn't in writing, it doesn't count in court. So, take notes at every meeting, review the notes with the franchisor, and have the franchisor initial the notes, to avoid any future misunderstandings.

#5 - Not knowing if you're ready to be self-employed. Unless you've already owned your own small business, the change to self-employment will put stress on your finances, your relationships with loved ones, and your feelings about yourself. Discuss these with those who matter to you before you leap.

#6 - Not carefully reading and understanding the franchise disclosure statement. The law requires that the franchisor give you a disclosure statement, at least 10 days before you sign up. However, there is no law that says that you have completely understood it. Check out the information with those who presently own a franchise.

#7 - Not getting good legal advice before you sign. Notice, it says before you sign, not after. After is too late. Go to a good franchise

Appendix B

attorney, not to the family lawyer, not to a real estate lawyer, not to a divorce lawyer.

#8 - **Failure to do enough market research.** You need to check out the demographics of the market, how many competitors there are and are likely to be, and whether you can have the right of first refusal on all future franchise locations in your area. Remember, the franchisor is not in the business you are going into; he is in the franchise selling business, so beware of what you are told about the market. Check it out.

#9 - **Not talking enough to other franchisees about franchise failures.** Many others failed because of reasons other than franchisor-caused failure. But maybe not; maybe it was all the fault of the franchisor. Ask other owners of this franchise about lawsuits, about the causes of failure of other owners, then ask the franchisor about it too.

#10 - **Not talking to enough other franchisees. They are your best source of information.** Talk to as many as you can, before you sign up. Take notes, ask all the questions you have on a written list of questions to ask them. Preparation in advance is the key to avoiding mistakes.

#11 - **Underestimating the time it will take to break even.** No matter how sharp you are, and no matter how good business is, it usually takes a bit longer than you expected. So, plan for this.

#12 - **Not having a complete enough understanding of the fees involved and the purchases you'll be required to make from the franchisor.** This is critical, because there is always the temptation to want to get the best deal you can on things, and you may be required to buy it from the franchisor, at a cost that is not the best deal. Be careful about this.

Tips for Prospective Franchise Buyers

1. When you meet with the franchisor, meet with someone at the management level, not just the in-house franchise salesperson or an outside franchise- marketing firm; they have too much to gain in commissions to always tell you the straight answers.

2. Check with the Better Business Bureau in the state where the franchise has its corporate offices.

3. Request from the franchisor a copy of its most recent 1-K registration filing; this will provide you with much more detailed information than what the disclosure statement has given you.

4. Before you sign, hire an attorney experienced in franchise law to review all the paperwork. The State Bar Association or the International Franchise Association in Washington D.C. can make a referral.

5. Contact the Attorney General's office in the state where the franchisor maintains corporate offices to see if there are any pending legal actions.

6. Be sure to insist on a strict completion date for any build-outs for the franchise, with a weekly compensation to you if stalls or delays occur.

Appendix B

7. Try to lower the initial franchise fee, which may be negotiable. If the fee is now higher than it used to be, try to get it at the original fee.

8. Ask for the same interest rate the franchisor gets on its loans.

9. Watch out for companies pushing a "starter kit" that will make you rich.

10. Watch out for franchise companies that make their money primarily from the sale of equipment, like laundry, dry cleaning, car wash, and printing.

11. Watch out for companies that want you to buy goods from the franchisor so you can "manufacture" them into a finished product.

12. Watch out for vending machine deals.

13. Remember, there are many advantages to buying a franchise, and for each, there is also a disadvantage. Be careful and be thorough.

Appendix C

10 Myths About Owning a One Person Business

Myth #1 I can live with little or no money *Oh yeah?*

Myth #2 I'll be my own boss *No, your customer is your new boss*

Myth #3 I'll get rich quick *Hope so*

Myth #4 I'll have more free time *You're joking*

Myth #5 I can live off of the business *Ah, but at what level?*

Myth #6 Running a business is easy *Some are, some aren't*

Myth #7 Owning a business is easy *Some are, but not most*

Myth #8 My excitement about it will sustain itself *Like living on love?*

Myth #9 My technical knowledge is all I need *What about doing marketing, sales, administration, and finance?*

Myth #10 The other 9 myths don't apply to me; think again! *Whoa!*

Which of the above myths had you already figured out to be myths? They are <u>all</u> myths, so think about the ones you think are not; ask yourself why you are in denial about those. Is it because you want don't them to be true? Well, they are. This is exactly why the three D's I mentioned in the introduction are important. Desire-Determination-Discipline.

Appendix D

11 Reasons Why Small Business Marketing Often Fails

Reason #1 - Forgot to create a niche - You tried to market to everybody. There is no "everybody". No niche, no results. A niche is a space in the mind of the prospects that have been targeted. It makes prospects choose your company instead of the competition.

Reason #2 - Ineffective newspaper ads - You spent too much and relied too much on newspaper ads. Of all of the types of street-smart marketing, newspaper ads have the worst results, compared to other forms of marketing. You need to cross-test them against other forms.

Reason #3 - Inattention to the demographics of prospective buyers -

Unless you know the mental and emotional needs of your prospects, how can you design a good marketing program to reach them in a way that will get them to take action? This will be just throwing your marketing dollars into the wind.

Reason #4 - Advertising companies have a different goal - Often the advertising company is more interested in winning awards for the ads than being focused on the results of your marketing. The ad that wins an award is not necessarily the ad that brings the most customers to you.

The One Person Business

Reason #5 - No call to action - If you haven't told the prospect exactly what you want him/her to do then how can they take the action you want them to take?

Many phone calls or ads or letters leave this out. That is a big mistake.

Reason #6 - No focus on benefits - Instead of having a focus on the benefits to the buyer, the marketing is focused on the features of the product/service. Features come later, after the benefits have been presented.

Reason #7 - Inconsistent with your positioning strategy - The strategy you use to position your company in the marketplace has to be reflected in the rest of your marketing. If it's not then you will be working and spending against yourself.

Reason #8 - Market target not well defined - Vague is not good. You need to narrow it down, target it to specific types, groups, areas, etc.

Reason #9 - Target not large enough - If your target market is too small you will not generate the volume you need (unless you sell a very expensive item that has a huge profit margin). You have to balance this with #8.

Reason #10 - The prospects are not reachable. What good is your marketing program if it doesn't reach the target, or if it costs much too much to reach it?

Reason #11 - Many targets, one message - You have such a great message and you use it to every target. Not good. Each target must have its own message.

Appendix E

8 Website Mistakes to Avoid

In the business world these days it is necessary for almost all businesses to have a website. The design is important; the message, the content is important; the user-friendliness is important. This means that you need to pay close attention to all three of those. If any one of them is poor your business will suffer. After all, your website is probably the first impression of your business that the viewer will get.

Here are eight mistakes you will want to avoid:

1. **The content is not pitched to your specific target.** If you have widely different targets you may need two websites, or two landing pages on one website.

2. **The page(s) is too busy. Keep it simple.** Make it as user/reader friendly as possible. (see Appendix Q)

3. **You forgot to tell them what you want them to do; this is called your 'call to action'.** Put it on every page of your website.

4. **You spent too much or too little on your website.** Doing it yourself using templates can save money, but it may end up costing you a lot in lost sales. On the other hand, some businesses do not need a fancy website with all the bells and whistles. Think this through carefully.

5. **. You forgot to update your website.** The content is not current in terms of your products or pricing or promotions. Review your site at least once a month. If you blog, do a blog at least once a week.

6. **You did too much of your website yourself.** Hiring someone, or using someone who knows how to do it, is a good idea. Design is a talent; writing content is a talent; management of the site is a skill. Think about this.

7. **It isn't mobile compatible.** Most websites are not, and in this new cyber world they need to be. Make sure your site can be read on a smart phone.

8. **It doesn't navigate.** Maybe the buttons are not working. Check them periodically to avoid frustrating and/or losing your prospective customer.

Appendix F

10 Traps That You Need to Avoid

Trap #1 - Picking a business with your head, not your heart

Of course you need to use your head, but not at first. At first you use your heart to see if you really love it.

Are you excited about the idea, passionate about it? Put off thinking about the profit margins, the location, the clients, the customers, the employees. That comes after you decide that you love it (or you don't). Will you feel joy? Will you feel proud of it?

Trap #2 - Emphasizing Product instead of People.

Many very successful businesses have lousy products and do very well. The quality may be low, but the service is great; the volume is high because lots of people want it where it is being sold. People buy value, they do not buy products. Value is created in many ways that may have nothing to do with the product. They perceive that it will make them feel good, look good, impress others, it's convenient, its familiar, it's supportive, it's reliable, whatever. It fills their emotional needs. Mainly, value is a relation between price and quality and features.

Trap #3 - Confusing Marketing and Sales

The One Person Business

Many small business owners try to sell while marketing. A big mistake. Marketing is to get your company name recognition, to position it well in the marketplace, to introduce something new, or in a new way. Marketing is presenting an offer to targeted prospects. It is done to get the phone to ring. Selling is to move the prospect from being a prospect to being a buyer. They take different strategies, different approaches. Sometimes marketing and sales happen piggyback, but they are still different.

Trap #4 - No Marketing Niche

Unless you limit your target you are trying to market to everybody. That doesn't work. The marketplace is very big and until and unless you create a niche for your company in that big marketplace you will not get good results. Many businesses try to use price and only price as a niche. That is not the way to go about it.

Trap #5 - Not Getting Enough Support

You own your business. You are alone. You bear the weight of the responsibility. You sign the checks.

You can get support from a community service organization, or your local SBDC office, or from friends, or an owner in a non-competing business. Ask for the support you need. Remember, you need it, so get it.

Trap #6 - Thinking that You Are Your Business

Too many small business owners think of it as their "child". They are much too ego involved with it. They can't see it as separate, a thing, an entity to be nurtured, grown, and then sold. This causes them to put the business first, before their family, their friends, and their own mental health. They think that if the business fails that they have failed. Pretty soon they hear people telling them to "get a life!" You have become a workaholic. Not good.

Trap #7 - The Business is Out of Balance

Not all parts of a small business have equal value to the business. Many owner spend too much time doing the work of the business and not enough doing the entrepreneurial part of it. Most owners spend too little time on marketing. Marketing drives everything else and should receive a

Appendix F

disproportionate share of the owner's time. To give equal time to sales, marketing, administration, finance and operations is to throw your business out of balance.

Trap #8 - You Run a Business with Negative Indicators

Suppose your sales are sufficient, customers are happy, you have a good location, lots of repeat business, things are well organized and well managed, but all is not well. Why not? Because you are in a counter-trend situation. The industry itself if going down hill; new technology is replacing your product little by little; your ratios are scary. Not good.

You have to have a business that goes with the trend, not against it. You need to sell the business or change it to bring in new products/services.

Trap #9 - Not Enough Testing and Tracking

To test for results, to measure and track the results is absolutely critical. Then the results must be paid attention to, not denied because you don't like them. Without enough testing/tracking you may think things are better than they are, OR, just as bad, you may think they are worse than they are. Either way, you lose.

Trap #10 - No Back-End Sales

Many business owners market well to get new customers and ignore marketing to existing and/or prior customers. It is less expensive to market to them. Your chances getting them to buy again are high. To ignore them is to ignore a very valuable potential.

Appendix G

36 Idea-Checkers to Assess Viability of Your Idea

You now have arrived at the key question, "Will this idea I've come up with really work?" I'm going to show you how to tell to a pretty high degree of predictability. To "work" means that it will be fun for you to do, it will make money, and it will be a positive influence on the other parts of your life.

No idea for a business is good or bad in and of itself. It may be good for one person and not for another. It depends upon the life and business experiences of the person, through which they filter the factors used here to do the evaluation of the business idea.

One person may put more weight on one of the "idea-checkers" and another person will think that it's not that important. So, remember, that <u>any evaluation of any business idea should be done by you for you</u>; not for anybody else, or by anybody else for you. Sure, you can discuss it afterwards, but <u>you</u> have to do it.

Also, it's obvious that if a business idea rates extremely low, it's probably because it's just one of those kind of ideas that would not have a chance no matter who was starting the business. Some ideas will have a greater chance of success no matter who starts up the business.

The One Person Business

How to Rate the Idea

Step 1. Assign to each factor a point score of 1 to 3. A score of 3 means it has a lot of that factor going for it; a 2 means it has some of it; a 1 means it has very little or none. Use the form at the end of this to put your ratings on.

Step 2. After you've rated all 36 factors, add up the total points.

Step 3. Divide the total points by 108 to get the percent of the points possible.

Step 4. Put a check-mark by any factor(s) that scored 2 or 1 point. Review them, as they are a caution to you.

See rating form below

A low score is a warning, not a death sentence. No business idea is going to be perfect. Any business idea might make money, but this Idea-Checker gives you a good idea as to which idea has the best potential to do so.

Even a high score will not guarantee success, but it is more likely to lead to it. If you are looking for an absolute guarantee, don't go into any business. There is always some risk.

Factor #1 - DOES IT EXCITE YOU? Will you love to do it, talk about it, and be happy with it? Rate it high if you will.

Factor #2 - CAN YOU LEVERAGE IT? this means, can you create it one time and be paid for it over and over again. Can it pay you while you sleep? Can you use other people's time, money, labor and brainpower to make money for you, rather than your own? Could it make money for you even after you sold the business?

Factor #3 - BIG POTENTIAL FOR INCOME? Some types or kinds of businesses make more money than others. How high is the bar of limitations on how much this business can earn for you. If your idea is to open a lemonade stand on the corner, rate it low.

Appendix G

<u>Factor #4</u> - ARE THE MARGINS HIGH? What makes the margins high is low cost of labor, low cost of materials, and low overhead expense, coupled with a nice high sales price.

<u>Factor #5</u> - IS THE INDUSTRY A HIGH GROWTH INDUSTRY? Is it on the upswing, rather than dying out? Are new customers coming to it? Is the marketplace for it growing?

<u>Factor #6</u> - DOES IT SOLVE A REAL PROBLEM? Will you be selling a product or service that provides a solution to a problem that lots of people have? Do they need what you will sell, or just want it?

<u>Factor #7</u> - IS IT SENSITIVE TO PRICE? You want the customer to perceive it as being worth a lot, even though it might not cost must to make it or provide it. If perception drives the price, rate it high. If it's desperately needed, or very unusual, or hard to get it will be much less price sensitive.

<u>Factor #8</u> - ARE THERE LOW START-UP COSTS? There is no correlation between how much it might earn down the road and how high the start-up costs are. Lower start-up costs means less investment and thus less risk.

<u>Factor #9</u> - WILL YOUR PERSONAL SKILLS AND TALENTS BE ABLE TO BE USED? You would not want to hire someone else to do what you can do really well. It is not good if the business will not use your best talents.

<u>Factor #10</u> - IS THERE A WELL-DEFINED MARKET? Is it easy to tell who will be your potential customers? Can you easily find out demographics about them. Is the market target clear?

<u>Factor #11</u> - CAN IT RIDE A TREND? It's much easier to go with a trend than to buck one. The momentum of the trend will bring in sales.

<u>Factor #12</u> - CAN YOU START IT PART-TIME? Can you keep that day job? This will keep some income coming in and reduce your risk.

<u>Factor #13</u> - IS IT A RELATIVELY "BIG TICKET" ITEM? The fewer the number of customers you have to create, the better. If the product or service has high value, and can thus bring a high price, it will take less people

The One Person Business

to produce and deliver it, and bring in large volumes of money and send out small volumes of product.

Factor #14 - ARE THE OPERATING COSTS LOW? If your overhead is too high, due to high fixed expenses or high variable expenses, your bottom line will suffer.

Factor #15 - CAN YOU TEST YOUR IDEA INEXPENSIVELY? You have to test out your advertising, your marketing, your hiring, your training, etc. Can these things be done without paying out too much to do them?

It's good if you can test out the feasibility of your idea for fewer bucks.

Factor #16 - WILL IT HAVE GOOD CASH FLOW? Some businesses have lots of sales and still go under, because they are owed too much money and can't collect it. Cash flow is king, and if you get paid in cash that's the best.

Factor #17 - IS THERE NOT MUCH COMPETITION? It's best to not be the first to enter the arena, but it's not good to be the last either. Fewer competitors make it a lot easier.

Factor #18 - IS IT EASILY CHANGED? Markets change, conditions change. A good thing it is when you can adapt easily to the changes, to go with the flow of events.

Factor #19 - DO CUSTOMERS COME BACK? Repeat business means lower marketing costs. It is lots easier to find a new product or service to provide for a customer than it is to find a new customer. It's good if a product gets used up quickly, so they need to buy more.

Factor #20 - NEEDS FEWER EMPLOYEES? Any time you get up over 7 or 8 employees the problems increase a lot. The fewer people you need to hire, train, manage, fire, and provide benefits for, the better.

Factor #21 - IS IT NEWSWORTHY? Getting a story about your company in the paper is like gold. Free publicity is the best kind. Can you get on talk shows to speak about it?

Factor #22 - WILL YOU NEED TO MAKE REPAIRS? The fewer the better. You then spend less time, money and energy, and you need to carry less inventory. Unless you want to open a service center as an additional profit center, avoid having to make repairs.

Factor #23 - ARE PRODUCT COSTS AND SUPPLIES CONSISTENT? It's important to always be able to purchase the supplies you need and materials you need. Can you get them, and is the price pretty stable? Are there lots of sources from which to get them?

Factor #24 ARE THERE UNIONS? They take up your time, your money, and can be a big hassle. To some workers unions are very important. But you're not the worker, you're the owner.

Factor #25 - ARE DELIVERY COSTS LOW? Is your product heavy and cost you a lot to ship it? Will you need a lot of equipment to move it around?

Factor #26 - IS IT ESTABLISHED? There are four combinations, going from best to worst. Best: sell a proven product in an existing market. Next best: sell a new product in an existing market. More risky: sell an existing, proven product in a new market. Worst: sell a new product in a new, unproven market.

Factor #27 - NEED MUCH INVENTORY? The more inventory you have to carry, the more cash you tie up, the more space you need to store it.

Factor #28 - HARD TO GET INTO THIS BUSINESS? It's good if entry into this business is difficult. It will keep others from becoming your competitors. Maybe it takes a lot of money, or education, or expertise. That's good, if you have those.

Factor #29 - WILL IT LAST? Will it go out of style or become obsolete quickly? You want a business that will be around for a long time.

Factor #30 - IS THE MARKET BIG ENOUGH? Even if your product is truly wonderful or your service is superb, you need to have a potential market that has enough people in it to produce enough sales. Selling surfboards in Kansas is not so good.

Factor #31 - IS IT SEASONAL? If all our sales come in one month or one quarter or one holiday, or depend on the weather, you will need very large cash reserves and be more at risk. The less dependent on those things, the better.

Factor #32 - CAN YOU EASILY SELL THE BUSINESS? You often make more money selling a business, after you've built it, than you would running it. You want a business that can build up equity and/or create a spin-off business from it. Then you can sell it profitably.

Factor #33 - IS THE LIABILITY RISK LOW? Some businesses draw lawsuits, while others never do. Lawsuits can put you out of business or, at minimum, cost you a fortune in liability insurance. Who needs it?

Factor #34 - WILL THERE BE ADD-ONS AND/OR UPGRADES? If you will have lots of different things to sell to your customers, as time goes on, that's good. If you have upgrades to sell them, that's good. Back-end sales mean bigger profits.

Factor #35 - NO GOVERNMENT INVOLVED? The less you have to deal with inspectors, regulators, committees, licenses and codes, the better. They drain your time, money, and energy.

Factor #36 - NO 'EXPERT' NEEDED? If your business totally depends on a highly trained or highly knowledgeable expert, that's not good. He may quit, or get sick, or die, or leave town. You want your business to be dependent on the systems you have put in place, not on people. Systems dependent is always better than people dependent.

Many of the 36 Idea Checkers will not apply to a one person business, However, if you think you might build the business and need employees sooner, rather than later or never, pay attention to all of the 36.

I wish you great good fortune as you explore ideas for starting your business. There is no guarantee, but I hope these ideas lead you on that path.

Rating Your Business Idea-Checker Form

Type of Business or Idea_____

Appendix G

Rate each factor 1 to 3.

1. Does it really excite you? ____

2. Can you leverage it? ____

3. Big potential for income? ____

4. Are the gross margins high? ____

5. Is the industry high growth? ____

6. Does it solve a real problem? ____

7. Is it low in sensitivity to price? ____

8. Are there minimal start-up costs? ____

9. Are your personal skills & talents to be used? ____

10. Is there a well-defined market? ____

11. Can you ride a current trend? ____

12. Can you start it part-time? ____

13. Is it a "big ticket" item? ____

14. Are the operating costs low? ____

15. Will it have good cash flow? ____

The One Person Business

16. Can you test your idea for just a little money? ____

17. Is there little or no competition? ____

18. Is it easily changed? ____

19. Do/will customers come back? ____

20. Does it avoid needed lots of employees? ____

21. Is it newsworthy? ____

22. Little or no repairs? ____

23. Are product costs and supplies consistent? ____

24. Are there no unions? ____

25. Are the delivery costs low?

26. Has it been proven yet as a viable business? ____

27. Low need for inventory? ____

28. Easy to get into? ____

29. Will it last? ____

30. Is the market big enough? ____

31. Is it good year-around? ____

Appendix G

32. Can you sell it easily? ____

33. Has a low liability risk? ____

34. Are there add-ons possible? ____

35. Is there absence of government involvement? ____

36. Is there absence of need for 'experts'? ____

Rating: If a strong yes, put 3 If so-so, put 2   If a no, put 1
Total Points ____ out of 108 possible
% of total (total divided by 108) ____

Appendix

Appendix H

Getting It Started

Locating Your Business

Steps:

1. Determine your business objectives

2. Define your business (what does it do, sell, make, etc.)

3. Research the demographics (age, income, family size, education level, etc.) of your prospective customer (for retail) or clients (for service business).

This may be the most important decision you make. Here are 31 factors to consider, depending on the type of business you are starting. This is for retail and office located businesses.

1. You may not have done enough research before you committed to a location.

2. You may not have done, for retail, traffic pattern research for foot traffic and vehicle traffic; origin of traffic; destination of traffic; gender and age of traffic, stoplights, turn lanes, speed limit, etc.

3. How much will the location cost, to renovate, build-out, remodel?

4. How much it will cost compared to other locations?

5. Will the site intercept traffic (foot or vehicle) going to another store or office.

6. You may not have considered the location of psychological barriers like freeways, rivers, mountains, etc.

7. For an office location, you may have forgotten to look at tenant mix.

8. You may not have considered parking, weather (sun, rain, snow), ease of access, etc.

9. You may not have considered how businesses near yours will impact on yours, for good or bad).

10. Is the site vulnerable to unfriendly competition?

11. What are the population demographics in the area?

12. Are the demographics improving or decaying as a trend?

Appendix H

13. How much competition is there in the area?

14. Should you be located near your competitors or far from them?

15. You may have ignored the neighborhood your customers must drive through to get to you.

16. You may have ignored noise factors.

17. Is it good for night business or being there at night?

18. You may have forgotten to consider social class factors.

19. Is there an adequate labor pool to draw from to get employees

20. Is there adequate police and fire protection?

21. Is good signage available?

22. Will crime insurance be too expensive?

23. Will pick up or delivery be easy?

24. Is it near where you live?

25. Is public transportation available near it?

26. Are customer rest rooms available?

27. If in a shopping center, where is it in the center?

28. How much space do you need now and potentially in the future.

29. What is the local business climate in the area?

30. What is the tax burden?

31. What are the wage/salary rates in the area?

Here are two tips.

1. Decide on objective factors, not on emotions.

2. When you are not sure, don't commit. "When in doubt, don't".

If you plan to do a home-based business you will still need to get zoning approval. This is not hard to get, but there are some typical restrictions, such as:

- No signs are permitted

- No displays or sale of merchandise

- No more than one employee who is not a bona fide resident of the dwelling may be employed or perform work on the premises

- No more than 20 cubic feet are permitted for storage of merchandise and materials

- No storage of contracting equipment or materials except in a commercial vehicle and no loading or unloading on the property

Appendix H

- **No more than 12 students or clients served per day and no more than four persons at any one time.**

There are other limitations that apply to some home occupations. Be sure to check with the Zoning Office of your jurisdiction for a complete and accurate listing of all conditions affecting home occupations before you make a decision to proceed with operating a business in your home.

Appendix I

Startup Costs*

    Deposits for utilities
    Capital Equipment costs-machines, fixtures, vehicles…
    Legal services
    Licenses & Permits
    Advertising
    Promotion
    Prepaid Insurance
    Salary or Draw of owner
    Labor (worker's wages)
    Rent
    Supplies
    Shipping costs
    Telephone
    Interest on Loan
    Build-out costs
    Security Deposit
    Grand Opening costs
    Cost of materials

The One Person Business

Cost of sales
Cost of initial inventory
Cost of build-out
Printing
Website creation
Website fees
Bank charges
Bookkeeping
Non-income taxes
* Not all will apply to your business

Appendix J

Direct Mail

Find out what your prospect's problem is and show him how your product or service will solve it. Sell the benefit and the solution. Your marketing plan and sales plan should focus on both of these.

In your marketing copy, use facts and figures instead of opinions. Use names, dates and places wherever possible. Above all, be honest.

Direct your message to one person, not to all. Keep the tone personal. Remove the adjectives and hyperboles, they create disbelief in the reader. Use short paragraphs, short sentences, and short words. Do not talk over their heads or beneath their dignity.

If you use direct mail marketing, a letter gets 70% of your orders, a brochure gets 20%, the order form gets 10%, but none of them get anything if your envelope doesn't get opened. To be a success, direct mail should bring in 2.2 times what you spent on the mailing. Repeat mailings are needed, since your audience forgets within two weeks 90% of what they see. You can create preferential uniqueness and separate yourself from your competitors in many ways: faster delivery, on-site services, gift wrapping, more frequent follow-up, a longer guarantee, more training, better shipping, free gifts, etc. You must find some way to gain a competitive advantage (CA). If you are in a business or market with a lot of competition, focus your marketing solely on your competitive advantage.

When your prospects compare you with your competition they will look at the following: perception that you are better, different, and/or going to benefit from doing business with you. Do they believe what you are telling them in your marketing? Are they being motivated to buy now or soon?

Your headline is the key to it all. Spend time creating a winning headline. Test and track different headlines. You only have three seconds to capture their attention. It's in the headline or not at all. A headline must interest the reader to want to learn more. Here are some ways to do that:

- **Speak directly to the reader**

- **Try headlines that begin with "New" or announce something**

- **Put a date in your headline**

- **Announce a free offer**

- **Start to tell a story**

- **Begin with "How to" or "How" or "What" of "Which" or "You" or "This"**

- **Maybe use a one word headline**

The United States Postal Service has program called Every Door. You can send a flyer to every home in a selected postal route in a selected postal zip code. The cost is only 16¢ per home. Check it out. They have a packet explaining it available at your local post office.

Appendix K

Marketing Plan

Your marketing strategy is <u>what</u> you plan to do. Your marketing plan is about <u>how </u>you plan to do what you plan to do. It is the implementation of your marketing strategy.

Your marketing strategy is about long term goals, targets, niches, trends, etc.

Your marketing plan is more specific; about timing, messages, calendar, budgets, mediums, etc.

1. **Keep it free of too much detail. Cover all bases, but avoid excess detail.**

2. **Keep it simple, uncluttered.**

3. **Let it be a problem solving process; this will clarify issues and solve problems.**

4. **It has to focus on the 6 key elements of marketing:**

The One Person Business

1) people 2) product 3) place 4) promotion 5) package 6) price

While different types of businesses will emphasize different ones of the six, every business must pay attention to and plan for all six. Base your marketing plan on your average prospect/customer, not the dumbest.

Part 1 - Summary

1. Talk about level of demand in your industry

2. Tell what you have to do to be successful in your market

3. Tell about the targets you have selected

4. Tell about how you will reach them

1. Tell about how you will meet the competition

2. Tell about your marketing mix of the six elements

Part 2 - Current Marketing Situation

1. Describe your market and its demographics

2. Talk about the geographic area

3. Give detail about the demographics

4. Tell how you will sell to each target

5. Describe the competition in each target market; be as detailed as you can

Appendix K

6. Provide an analysis of your competition.

Their market share
Their advertizing
Their pricing strategies
Their distribution/delivery system
How long in business?
Are they heavy in debt?
What are their target markets?
Do they compete on price, quality, service, or convenience?
Describe your competitive advantage (CA)

Part 3 - Threats and Opportunities

1. Describe any threats in your industry or from your competition.

2. Describe any threats in the general economy-interest rates, loan funds, etc.

3. Describe the opportunities in your target markets for new products, new services, etc.

Part 4 - Objectives and Issues

1. Tell your goals for each market target

2. Tell what are the challenges, problems, issues you face in your markets?

Part 5 - Marketing Strategy

1. Tell your strategy in general

2. Tell about your market niche(s)

3. Tell about specific strategy for each target market

4. Tell how it is consistent with your sales process

Part 6 - Plan for Action

1. Provide your marketing calendar

2. Provide your marketing budget

3. Name the controls (testing and tracking) you will use

Appendix L

49 Tips and Checklist for Retail Startup

1. What terms do your suppliers offer you?

2. What systems do you have for inventory turnover and inventory re-order?

3. Who will reconcile your bank statements?

4. What financial statements will you (or your accountant) generate each month?

5. Are your receivables, if you have any, current?

6. What system do you have for collecting receivables?

7. Can you keep your shrinkage (bad debt, internal loss and external loss) at less than 2%?

8. Is your lease competitive, renewable, and are the terms favorable to you?*

9. Is your payroll (if any) an acceptable percentage of your sales revenue?

10. Do your financial ratios correspond favorably with industry standards?

11. Is your signage effective and informative?

12. Is your store ready for business when it is opened?

13. Is everything clean and in good working order?

14. Will your window displays change regularly?

15. Do you have operation systems?

16. Can you describe your target customer in two or three sentences?

17. How will your customers be greeted upon entering your shop?

18. How will your phone be answered?

19. Will your merchandizing (purchasing, display, signage, pricing, payment policies, and returns) be made from a customer service perspective?

20. What will be your follow-up system with customers?

Appendix L

21. What will be your marketing plan?

22. How much do you know about your competition's pricing, policies, marketing?

23. What, if any, discounts, sales, "loss leaders" will you have?

24. Who will have keys, access to the money, etc.?

25. Do you have a fire extinguisher and first aid kit on site?

26. Are your emergency numbers posted in front and rear of store?

27. Are any dressing rooms monitored by staff?

28. Are stockroom and office doors closed and secure?

29. Will you conduct regular inventory 'spot checks' on costly goods?

30. Will you have a computerized Point of Sale system that provides effective data and control?

31. Will the Point of Sale system integrate with your accounting and inventory systems?

32. Will your business have a website (it should)?

33. Will you match packing slips with purchase orders and with invoices?

34. Will you make bank deposits daily?

35. What will be your policy for damaged or spoiled goods?

36. Will the amount of your inventory support your sales system?

37. Do you know your inventory in detail?

38. Do you markdown items in a timely and well-promoted fashion?

39. Is your merchandize clean, well displayed, grouped, accessible, well lighted, and restocked throughout the day?

40. Differentiate Your Business

Be one or more of these: the only - the first - the best - widest selection - the hippest - most convenient - best people - the newest - most value

41. Make your store:

   a. the most unique - stability in hours open - a great experience – clean great lighting - good signage - addresses traffic- street or pedestrian

   b. change windows on a schedule

   c. change store layout on a schedule

   d. optimize customer traffic flow inside your store. Remember, retail is theater; give your customer a great experience.

Appendix L

42. Use track and spot lighting, not fluorescent

43. Your website (and you need to have one) must include: home page about us content contact us

44. Renegotiate with your lenders and/or your vendors and/or your landlord

45. Remember, profit is an opinion; cash is a fact

46. Turn your inventory at least twice a year; after one year, sell it off at cost

47. Keep your rent as close as possible to 10% of your annual sales

48. One testimonial is worth 200 TV ads

49. Your marketing budget should be 5% to 15% of your gross sales.

* Before you sign your lease, know about these: (for retail or office leases)

Location - Does it fit your budget?
Tenant mix - Who else is in the building?
Size Square feet - How many walls can be moved?
Renewals - Do you have the right to renew the lease?
Maintenance - Who pays for what to maintain the property? Any CAM fee?
Terms - These can be as important as the price.
Build-out - Who pays for what? Who picks the quality?
Out Clause - If possible, have it say you can get out after X months.

The One Person Business

Signage - Where, how big, what kind?

Parking - Free? How many spaces, where, reserved?

Non-compete - A clause that says the landlord cannot rent in the building to a business that would compete with what you sell.

Guarantees - Are any of the representations made by the landlord or his agent guaranteed; like foot traffic count, like is the key tenant staying?

Net - Is it a triple net lease or what?

Insurance - What is needed, what is not needed?

<u>Tips:</u> Everything in a lease is negotiable –everything!

Until it is signed, during negotiations, if the other side wants to change <u>anything</u> in the lease, then every other item in the lease is then open for further negotiation.

Appendix M

Types of Customers

There are at least two different ways to think about the different types or kinds of customers you have. The first is to describe the different motivations a prospect may have.

Best deal: Get a good deal; price is most important.

Big lots: These shoppers want to buy in large quantities.

Detailed: They want to see all the facts and compare and contrast.

Bonded: These people want an ongoing relationship with either the owner or the business.

Status: They are mostly interested in what others will think of them.

Another way to categorize prospects is by their personality types: There are four types of "Emotional Hot Buttons" that motivate your prospects/customers to purchase: Needs, Wants, Fears and Anxieties; people want to get one or more of these satisfied. Your marketing should promise to satisfy at least one of these four. Your sales process should identify which it is and speak to it.

(1) NEEDS are things that you think you must have. The prospect/customer thinks he or she must have it to satisfy one or more of the categories mentioned in the first way, the categorizations up above this.

(2) **WANTS are things which you don't need to have, but would really like to have.** Your marketing should promise to satisfy one or more of these.

(3) **DESIRES are those things you wish for, hope for. They are like back-burner wants.** Your marketing should promise to fulfill at least part of them.

(4) **ANXIETIES are the things we feel uncomfortable with, that make us uneasy.** Your marketing should promise to relieve the anxiety. Sometimes it's a good idea to create a little anxiety and then relieve it.

What are you really selling?

You may think you're selling bonds or homes or landscaping, or hamburgers. But if your answer involves mentioning your product's features, you don't know what you're really selling!

Razor companies know that they don't sell blades. They sell comfort. Cosmetic companies know they don't sell lipstick. They sell romance. To figure out what you are really selling, which is what they are really buying, remember that you must satisfy one or more of those four emotional hot buttons. People buy emotionally and then rationalize the decision to buy in their intellect. In most people, most of the time, emotion dominates thinking, and this applies to buying decisions. Have you ever gone into a store, bought something you had no intention of buying, and then given yourself reasons why it was a good idea to buy it as you walked out of the store? Most of us have.

Appendix N

Tracking Your Results

These are the most important things to keep track of in your business. Since types of businesses vary, no business will use all of them.

A new business, just starting up, should track many of these from the first day.

If you don't track things you won't know what is going on in your business. Set up the tracking systems <u>before</u> you open for business.

Your Market

1. How many people are in your market target?

2. What percent of the target was reached?

3. How many leads did it generate?

4. How many appointments did it generate?

5. What percent of the leads made an appointment?

The One Person Business

<u>Sales</u>

1. How many sales resulted from the appointments?

2. What percent of the appointments became sales?

3. What was the average dollar amount of the sales?

<u>Response Rates</u> (to direct mail or telemarketing)

1. How many direct mail pieces or telemarketing phone calls were sent/made?

2. What percent of them resulted in an appointment?

<u>Store Traffic</u>

1. How many customers came in to the store?

2. What percent of those actually bought something?

3. What was the average dollar spent by each customer?

4. What time of day did they buy?

5. What day of the week did they buy?

<u>Advertising Tracking</u>

1. How many people responded to the ad?

Appendix N

    2. How many sales did the ad generate?

    3. How many sales dollars did the ad generate?

    4. Did it pay for itself and then some?

<u>Telephone Inquiries</u>

1. What was the source that generated the call (ad, word-of-mouth, yellow pages, etc.)

2. For what reason did they call?

3. What data about them did you capture or not capture?

<u>Promotional Events (sale, trade show, seminar, etc.)</u>

1. How many people attended?

2. How many people contacted your table or booth?

3. How many sales were made or leads obtained?

4. What percent of the people who contacted your table/booth actually bought something or gave you sales lead data about themselves?

5. What was the average dollar amount they spent?

The One Person Business

<u>Marketing Handouts (brochures, flyers, business cards, giveaways, etc.)</u>

1. How many were given out?

2. How many responses did each generate?

3. What percent of responses did it generate?

<u>Customer Acquisition Costs</u>

1. How much marketing cost did it take to get the sale?

2. Divide the total cost of marketing and sales by the number of sales generated.

<u>Customer Satisfaction</u> (via customer survey or service evaluation cards)

1. How many compliments did your business get?

2. How many complaints did your business get?

3. How many items were returned?

4. What percent were returned?

<u>Finance- Track by dollar amount and by percent</u>

1. What are your profit margins?

2. How are your expenses trending?

Appendix N

3. How is your cash flow charting?

<u>Production</u> (If you sell a physical product)

1. How many were rejects?

2. How many needed to be re-done?

3. Is your inventory able to meet all order demand?

4. Are your orders fulfilled in a timely manner?

5. Is your inventory control system functioning well?

<u>Website Sales or Leads</u>

1. How many leads did your informational website generate?

2. How many of those leads were converted to a sale?

3. What was the average dollar of sales generated from each sale?

4. If you sell on the web, how many sales were made?

5. How many dollars did each sale generate, on average?

<u>The benefits of tracking are:</u>

1. You get reliable numbers on which to base your business decisions.

The One Person Business

2. **You will have more control over what is happening.**

3. **You can compare apples to apples.**

No tracking=no data no data=poor decisions. Your decisions should be driven by your numbers, which come from tracking.

Appendix O

Profit Margins Explained

Your profit margin is a ratio, expressed as a percentage. You use the numbers from your Income Statement to calculate them, which is also called your Profit & Loss Statement.

The gross margin represents the percent of total sales revenue that the company retains after incurring the direct costs associated with producing the goods and services sold by your company. Here is the formula:

Gross Profit Margin (%) = Total Revenue <u>minus</u> Cost of Goods Sold <u>divided by</u> Total Revenue. Cost of Goods Sold (COGS) is the total cost of your materials and labor) Calculate in some labor cost even if you are a one person business.

The net profit margin ratio (pre-tax) is your net income <u>divided by</u> your net sales. Net income is the total of all of your expenses, including taxes, interest expense, and depreciation. Your net sales number is your total sales less any returns or allowances.

These two ratios, gross profit margin and net profit margin are important for two reasons. First, you can compare them to the same average margins in your industry. Secondly, you can compare them to your own margins from months/quarters/years past and see how they trend.

The One Person Business

The bottom line here is that the two profit margins let you know if you are making any money or not. Good to know.

Appendix P

Writing a Business Plan to Start-Up, Buy, or Grow a Small Business

Before You Start Writing It:

1. Talk to people who are in the business you have picked

2. Talk to the professional advisors at your local SBDC office

3. Gather information about the industry your business is part of

4. Create the vision-type goals for your business

5. Set a time schedule for doing and completing the business plan

6. Limit it to 30 pages maximum. Some small businesses, especially one person businesses, do not need a full-blown business plan. A short version will suffice. This means that some of the sections in a full business plan will not be done, but do not neglect the marketing and financial sections.

The One Person Business

<u>Why Write One?</u>

1. **It helps you identify objectives**

2. **It helps you develop strategies to meet the objectives**

3. **It will red-flag problems and suggest ways to solve them**

4. **It will help you avoid future problems**

5. **It will start-off good management practices**

6. **It will give you a good idea about the money aspects**

7. **It will clarify whether or not your idea will work**

8. **It will let you know whether you are kidding yourself or not**

The best thing to do is to go online and find a good outline for a business plan. There are lots of them out there. The SBDC has a good one on-line at VASBDC.org. Try to find one that is annotated, that tells what each section of the plan should include.

Here are some general tips for writing a business plan:

<u>Tips</u>

1. **If you plan to submit your business plan to a bank it has to be formatted professionally. Remember, however, that most banks do not lend to startups.**

2. **Do not do the summary and mission statement until last.**

Appendix P

3. The items do not have to be done in order. Do the ones you feel/know the most about first.

4. Be as specific as you can. The more detail the better.

5. Every business needs some kind of business plan, but not all need it at the same point in the growth of the business. You cannot effectively manage a business if you have no plan.

6. If you need help with it contact your local Small Business Development Center (SBDC); it is free help and confidential.

For a one person business it may suffice to do a mini business plan. Here is a list of what it should include:

1. What is the mission, the purpose for which you are starting this business?

2. What will your business sell?

3. When and where will it operate?

4. What market research has been done?

5. What is your marketing strategy?

6. To whom will you market? (market target(s).

7. How will it reach each target?

8. What is your marketing message? (see #9)

The One Person Business

9. What is your competitive advantage (CA); what makes your business unique in the marketplace?

10. What is your marketing budget?

11. What is your marketing calendar?

12. What marketing materials and mediums will be used?

13. What is your company name, slogan, and logo?

14. What is your analysis of your competition?

15. What are any potential weaknesses of your business (money, competition, location, and so on).

16. How much money will you need?

17. Where will the financing come from?

18. What will be your startup costs? (this is part of #16)

19. What are your sales projections?

20. What are your budget projections?

21. What are your cash flow projections?

22. What is your breakeven point?

23. How will customers pay you?

Appendix P

24. Who will do the books?

25. What profit margins and ratios will you track?

26. What business legal entity will you use? (sole proprietor, LLC, S-P- C corporation)

27. What business insurance will you have?

28. What sales process will you use?

29. How will your product or service be delivered to the customer?

Each of the items to include in your mini business plan is discussed somewhere in this book. The emphasis here, for a mini plan, is on marketing and finance. Those are the key to getting a good start.

Appendix Q

Selling Online

It is not so easy to sell online, because there is a lot of competition and because most websites are not very good. Here are some tips:

1. It is better to try to sell just one or a few items on one site. Be sure to give a really good description of the product(s) or service, with a lot of customer benefits.

2. Use follow-up marketing to sell other products you have, or create an additional website.

3. Test test test. Track different products and different prices.

4. Offer a 'trade' where you give them a free gift of some kind in exchange for them giving you their email address so you can send it to them via email. It can be a story about your product, or the history of it, or uses for it, whatever.

5. Put the offer on your home page. Put it in the upper left corner, or at least above the scroll. Your entire home page should be above the scroll.

6. You can also put the 'trade' on every other page, or in a hover ad, which is like a pop-up.

7. Since your headline is the first thing they see on your website, be sure that it contains benefits for the customer, and/or a solution to a problem the customer has.

8. Put plenty of customer testimonials in your site. Be sure that they tell how your product/service helped them.

9. People want to deal with an expert, so put in as much good stuff about your credentials, background, and experience as you can.

10. Make the viewer think that he/she should buy right now by offering special deals for doing so.

11. Your website is really your sales letter. Use bold type in spots, use centering, use subheads, use different length paragraphs, use bullet lists.

12. Put in images and even a video.

13. Test and track different headlines, different copy content, different special offers.

Appendix R

Responses to Objections

What follows here takes courage to use. However, they are all time tested and they work. You will notice that when the prospect says something you respond with a question. Practice makes perfect.

Prospect Says "I'm not interested"

You say "That's just what I said when I heard about this, then I found out (give your main benefit)."

Prospect Says "Just send me some literature"

You say "That's exactly what I want to do, and I'll highlight what will be of most interest to you; tell me, what's the biggest frustration you're presently facing in your job/business?"

Prospect Says "I don't see any reason to change who I presently buy from."

You say "I can understand how you would feel that way; when I've been in your situation I've found out that there were some real differences that I wished I'd been aware of. For example, what are your greatest frustrations in the area of …"

Prospect Says "That's fantastic!"

You say "What do you like about it?"

Prospect Says "I have no interest in going any further with this."

The One Person Business

You say "Can you tell me why that is?"
Prospect Says "I told you, I'm not interested."
You say "You must be telling me that for a reason."
Prospect Says "Just give me your business card."
You say (look for it, but don't find it) Then say, "I assume you want it so you could call me. Why were you going to call me?"
Prospect Says "I really can't afford it."
You say "Which means?" or "Well, if you could afford it, then what?"
Prospect Says "This is too hard to remember all this stuff"
You say "Perhaps; but not as hard as not having the benefits it will bring you."
Prospect Says "You sure are asking a lot of questions."
You say "Yes, because I'm interested in seeing how I can best help you."
Prospect Says "I don't like this."
You say "I get the feeling you're upset. Can you tell me why?"
Prospect Says "I'll think it over."
You say "Tell me, please, why did you decide not to buy."
Prospect Says "I don't like the price."
You say "Off the record, what price are you looking for?"
Prospect Says "The price is just too high."
You say "I'd rather explain the reason for the price once than to have to explain poor quality many times."
Prospect Says "You sales guys always do this to me."
You say "Do this to me means…"
Prospect Says "I can get it for less from your competitor."
You say "Looks like I won't be getting the order then, huh?"
Prospect Says "Well, I don't have any money budgeted for this."
You say "So, how do you plan to pay for it?"
Prospect Says "It seems we have a problem here?"
You say "Do you see a way to overcome it?"
Prospect Says "I don't need any."

Appendix R

You say "If you were calling on me, instead of me calling on you, what would you do to get more of my business?"

Prospect Says "I like it, but I can't afford it."

You say "Here's my problem. Even if my product/service would solve all your problems, you can't afford it anyway."

Prospect Says something that leads away from a decision to buy

You say "You must be telling me that for a reason."

Prospect Says Prospect is putting up a lot of resistance to buying

You say "Tell me, why are you putting all this pressure on me?"

Do you really want to make the sale? Well then, practice using those responses and see what happens. I think you'll be pleasantly surprised. They simply hold up a mirror for the prospect to look into.

Appendix S

Service Business Tips

1. After you convert a lead and get the sale or installation of your product, there is a four part cycle that you want to keep in a flow. Sale»service»maintenance»replacement

2. Be sure to follow up on every proposal or quote.

3. Try to sell a maintenance agreement every time even a week after the sale.

4. Always have the sales rep, the estimator, or yourself give the prospective customer the price at the site, not on the phone. It's too easy for them to say no on the phone.

5. Give them more than they expect, then they will be a return customer.

6. After the job, always send a thank you note.

7. Keep a tickler file to remind you to do the follow-up.

8. 72 hours after completion of the work call and ask if everything is alright.

9. Put some marketing on the back side of your invoice or receipt.

10. Always get at least 10% down payment to lock them in.

11. If you have a maintenance agreement do this:
    1. Call to schedule the maintenance
    2. Call to confirm that you will be coming to perform maintenance
    3. Perform it to a high quality of workmanship
    4. Follow up within 24 hours with a phone call to make sure everything is alright
    5. Follow up every 90 days with a postcard or email.

Appendix T

Reasons to Do a Home-Based Business

1. There are a few possible tax benefits, but be careful.

2. You get to work at home and may save child-care costs, auto costs, etc.

3. It's cheaper than renting office space.

4. It takes less money to get started.

5. You don't have to work with people you might not like.

6. There will be fewer government regulations to deal with.

7. You can work any time of the day or night.

Reasons to Not Do a Home-Based Business

1. There may be zoning or other laws that prohibit it or restrict it too much.

2. There is a risk that your home life and business life will flow into each other.

3. You may not be enough of a self-disciplined person to stay focused.

4. The type of business you want to have may not lend itself to using your home to run it.

5. When the operational work of the business is done you may go do home-related work instead of doing the entrepreneurial work you should do for the business.

6. There may be many too many interruptions from your kids, neighbors, etc.

7. You may not be dedicated to it enough to have it prosper.

Appendix U

Tax Deductions for Business Expenses

There are two kinds of commonly deducted business expenses. This applies to whether you are a home-based business, a retail store, or an office-based business.

The first kind is called ordinary expenses. This must be something that happens in a particular kind of business. For example, gas expense if you have a limousine business.

The second kind is called necessary expenses. This is where an expense is needed to have or do in the business. For example, a plumber needs to have a pipe threading tool.

Promotion and advertising
Business related meals and entertainment
Professional fees
Conferences and continuing education classes
Office supplies
Use of car for business purposes
Business travel
Postage and shipping
Telephone, computer, printer

The One Person Business

Office equipment and tools
Tax preparation
Parking and toll fees
Business related magazines, reports, etc.

If you are in doubt about any of the items on the list, or any not on the list, talk to your tax preparation person or accountant. Remember, they have to be business related expenses, not personal expenses.

$$\Omega$$

www.ingramcontent.com/pod-product-compliance
Lightning Source LLC
Chambersburg PA
CBHW051643170526
45167CB00001B/310